Meet
the
Candidate
Videos

Recent Titles in the
Praeger Series in Political Communication
Robert E. Denton, Jr., *General Editor*

Meet
the
Candidate
Videos

Analyzing Presidential Primary Campaign Videocassettes

John H. Parmelee

Praeger Series in Political Communication

Westport, Connecticut
London

Library of Congress Cataloging-in-Publication Data

Parmelee, John H., 1970–
    Meet the candidate videos : analyzing presidential primary campaign videocassettes / John H. Parmelee.
        p. cm. — (Praeger series in political communication, ISSN 1062–5623)
        Includes bibliographical references and index.
        ISBN 0–275–97737–4 (alk. paper)
        1. Advertising, Political—United States.   2. Primaries—United States.   3. Video recordings—United States.   4. Communication in politics—United States.   5. Mass media—Political aspects—United States.   I. Title.
    II. Series.
    JF2112.A4 P285 2003
    324.273′0154—dc21   2002072804

British Library Cataloguing in Publication Data is available.

Library of Congress Catalog Card Number: 2002072804
ISBN: 0–275–97737–4
ISSN: 1062–5623

First published in 2003

Praeger Publishers, 88 Post Road West, Westport, CT 06881
An imprint of Greenwood Publishing Group, Inc.
www.praeger.com

Printed in the United States of America

The paper used in this book complies with the Permanent Paper Standard issued by the National Information Standards Organization (Z39.48–1984).

10 9 8 7 6 5 4 3 2 1

Contents

Series Foreword

Those of us from the discipline of communication studies have long believed that communication is prior to all other fields of inquiry. In several other forums I have argued that the essence of politics is "talk" or human interaction.[1] Such interaction may be formal or informal, verbal or nonverbal, public or private, but it is always persuasive, forcing us consciously or subconsciously to interpret, to evaluate, and to act. Communication is the vehicle for human action.

From this perspective, it is not surprising that Aristotle recognized the natural kinship of politics and communication in his writings *Politics* and *Rhetoric*. In the former, he established that humans are "political beings [who] alone of the animals [are] furnished with the faculty of language."[2] In the latter, he began his systematic analysis of discourse by proclaiming that "rhetorical study, in its strict sense, is concerned with the modes of persuasion."[3] Thus, it was recognized over twenty-three hundred years ago that politics and communication go hand in hand because they are essential parts of human nature.

In 1981, Dan Nimmo and Keith Sanders proclaimed that political communication was an emerging field.[4] Although its origin, as noted, dates back centuries, a "self-consciously cross-disciplinary" focus began in the late 1950s. Thousands of books and articles later, colleges and universities offer a variety of graduate and undergraduate coursework in the area in such diverse departments as communication, mass communication, journalism, political science, and sociology.[5] In Nimmo and Sanders's early assessment, the "key areas of inquiry" included rhetorical analysis, propaganda analysis, attitude change studies, voting studies, government and the news media, functional and systems analyses, technological changes, media tech-

nologies, campaign techniques, and research techniques.[6] In a survey of the
state of the field in 1983, the same authors and Lynda Kaid found additional, more specific areas of concern such as the presidency, political polls,
public opinion, debates, and advertising.[7] Since the first study, they have
also noted a shift away from the rather strict behavioral approach.

A decade later, Dan Nimmo and David Swanson argued that "political
communication has developed some identity as a more or less distinct domain of scholarly work."[8] The scope and concerns of the area have further
expanded to include critical theories and cultural studies. Although there
is no precise definition, method, or disciplinary home of the area of inquiry, its primary domain comprises the role, processes, and effects of
communication within the context of politics broadly defined.

In 1985, the editors of *Political Communication Yearbook: 1984* noted that
"more things are happening in the study, teaching, and practice of political communication than can be captured within the space limitations of
the relatively few publications available."[9] In addition, they argued that
the backgrounds of "those involved in the field [are] so varied and plural-
ist in outlook and approach, ... it [is] a mistake to adhere slavishly to any
set format in shaping the content."[10] More recently, Nimmo and Swanson
have called for "ways of overcoming the unhappy consequences of frag-
mentation within a framework that respects, encourages, and benefits
from diverse scholarly commitments, agendas, and approaches."[11]

In agreement with these assessments of the area and with gentle en-
couragement, in 1988 Praeger established the series entitled "Praeger Series in Political Communication." The series is open to all qualitative and
quantitative methodologies as well as contemporary and historical studies. The key to characterizing the studies in the series is the focus on communication variables or activities within a political context or dimension.
As of this writing, over 80 volumes have been published and numerous
impressive works are forthcoming. Scholars from the disciplines of communication, history, journalism, political science, and sociology have par-
ticipated in the series.

I am, without shame or modesty, a fan of the series. The joy of serving
as its editor is in participating in the dialogue of the field of political communication and in reading the contributors' works. I invite you to join me.

Robert E. Denton, Jr.

NOTES

1. See Robert E. Denton, Jr., *The Symbolic Dimensions of the American Presidency*
(Prospect Heights, IL: Waveland Press, 1982); Robert E. Denton, Jr., and Gary
Woodward, *Political Communication in America* (New York: Praeger, 1985; 2d ed.,
1990); Robert E. Denton, Jr., and Dan Hahn, *Presidential Communication* (New York:

Praeger, 1986); and Robert E. Denton, Jr., *The Primetime Presidency of Ronald Reagan* (New York: Praeger, 1988).

2. Aristotle, *The Politics of Aristotle*, trans. Ernest Barker (New York: Oxford University Press, 1970), p. 5

3. Aristotle, *Rhetoric*, trans. W. Rhys Roberts (New York: The Modern Library, 1954), p. 22.

4. Dan Nimmo and Keith Sanders, "Introduction: The Emergence of Political Communication as a Field," in *Handbook of Political Communication*, eds. Dan Nimmo and Keith Sanders (Beverly Hills, CA: Sage, 1981), pp. 11–36.

5. Ibid., p. 15.

6. Ibid., pp. 17–27.

7. Keith Sanders, Lynda Kaid, and Dan Nimmo, eds. *Political Communication Yearbook: 1984* (Carbondale: Southern Illinois University Press, 1985), pp. 283–308.

8. Dan Nimmo and David Swanson, "The Field of Political Communication: Beyond the Voter Persuasion Paradigm," in *New Directions in Political Communication*, eds. David Swanson and Dan Nimmo (Beverly Hills, CA: Sage, 1990), p. 8.

9. Sanders, Kaid, and Nimmo, *Political Communication Yearbook: 1984*, p. xiv.

10. Ibid.

11. Nimmo and Swanson, "The Field of Political Communication," p. 11.

Acknowledgments

This book, which explores a unique and previously unexplored area of political communication, would not have been possible without the assistance of many friends and colleagues. I would like to thank professors Marilyn Roberts, Bernell Tripp, Churchill Roberts, and Richard Conley for their guidance. In addition, Michelle Barth, Lori Boyer, Naeemah Clark, Kelly Page, and Aleen Ratzlaff also deserve recognition for their support. Access to the campaign videos was generously provided by several sources, including the University of Oklahoma Political Commercial Archives and the campaigns.

I am also grateful to the producers of the presidential primary campaign videocassettes for the 2000 race—Paul Curcio, Tom Edmonds, William Knapp, and Paul Sanderson—who took the time to talk with me about what function the videocassettes served in their campaign.

My love and gratitude go out to my wife, Amy, a copy editor by profession whose keen eyes made my manuscript a far more readable work.

Finally, James Sabin at Greenwood Publishing made sure the manuscript turned into a book.

Chapter One

The Significance of Presidential Primary Campaign Videocassettes

In the fall of 1991 an Arkansas governor, little known to the rest of the country, campaigned for president in the snow of New Hampshire. Though scandal had rocked his campaign, Bill Clinton and his young staff continued to wage an aggressive campaign using a variety of high-tech advertising techniques. One such strategy was to mail out 20,000 free videocassettes to undecided voters in New Hampshire highlighting Clinton's biographical background and stands on various issues.

The 16-minute video, titled "The New Covenant," visually and verbally focused on issues of change—change for America and for the Democratic Party. These themes remained consistent throughout Clinton's primary and general election campaigns. As he noted in one segment of the video, "There's a hole in our politics where our sense of common purpose used to be. But Democrats who want to change the government, who want the government to do more—and I'm one of them—we have a heavy responsibility to show that we're going to spend the taxpayers' money wisely and with discipline" (Clinton, 1991).

The last third of the video exemplifies Clinton's attempt to learn from what he says are the mistakes of past Democratic presidential nominees. "The American people already know what we're against, let's tell them what we're for," Clinton says as he introduces his 1992 agenda: health care reform, education initiatives, national service, and economic growth. By primary election day, 70% of those who received the video watched it (Devlin, 1994). Half of those who watched the video voted for Clinton (Ceaser and Busch, 1993). The video is one of the strategic tools credited with Clinton's "Comeback Kid" finish in New Hampshire.

PURPOSE OF THE STUDY

Presidential candidates have used these primary campaign "meet the candidate" videos since the 1980s, yet little academic research has tracked the videos' evolution as an advertising strategy or examined the videos' impact on voters. According to Mundy (1995), these videos, which generally provide biographical and issue information about the candidate, are "a hot secret among political consultants." She adds the following:

> Video ads avoid "media interpretation"—if the candidate babbles foolishly or ignores a serious question from the press, the friendly film editor fixes the faux pas and leaves you the best part. They are also extremely cheap to produce and mail— maybe $1.25 for a 10-minute slobberfest including tape, postage and a fundraising letter. That is a fraction of the cost of a prime-time advertising buy and, if it is executed properly, the video will generate free media coverage. (p. 22)

Presidential primary videos, which can run from 5 to 20 minutes, are marketed to potential donors and mailed to voters in key battleground states the candidate hopes to win. The videos also are shown by Democratic and GOP faithful at party functions (Faucheux, 1994, 1997; Luntz, 1988). The videocassettes are paid candidate advertising, which are produced by political advertising firms early in the presidential race. These paid political ads can cost more than $150,000 to produce and distribute (Washington Notebook, 1995).

Presidential primary campaign videocassettes can trace their beginnings to George Bush's 1980 presidential campaign (Sabato and Beiler, 1988, p. 8). By 1988, 11 of the 13 major presidential candidates had added direct mail videos to their primary campaign advertising strategy (Luntz, 1988, p. 211). Some campaigns mass mailed videos to all registered voters in their party in key states, while other candidates targeted videos to party activists (Norrander, 1988, p. 15). Print and broadcast journalists also are a target of the videos' messages: reporters receive candidate videos and often do stories on them (Carney, 1999; Connolly, 1999; Barone, 1995; Kurtz, 1995; Mundy, 1995; Thompson and Kuhnhenn, 1995; Rosenstiel, 1992; Luntz, 1988, p. 212; Blumenthal, 1987; Grove, 1987).

Presidential candidates recently experimented with using the Internet to disseminate their videos. For the 2000 race, Vice President Al Gore mailed out videotapes and also included the video on his presidential campaign web site, and Senator John McCain included a link on his web site to order copies of his video for $15. This technique increased the video's benefit as a fund-raising vehicle.

RESEARCH QUESTIONS

These "meet the candidate" videos are used by presidential hopefuls, not incumbents, during the early months of the primary season. For many presidential campaigns, its primary campaign videocassette is the first advertising distributed to voters. Looking at presidential primary campaign videocassettes allows those in political communication to explore the rhetorical and visual themes used by candidates to introduce themselves— or in some cases reintroduce themselves—to the American people.

One GOP political strategist, Greg Stevens, says presidential primary videocassettes are invaluable to candidates in primary campaigning: "Imagine hundreds of groups of 10 or more gathered in their living rooms, just watching one of these" (quoted in Mundy, 1995, p. 22). But what exactly are they watching? How are the candidates' images and issues framed in each videocassette? What function do the videocassettes serve in primary campaigning? The main research questions can be broken into three broad categories:

What are viewers watching in these presidential primary campaign videocassettes? The longer nature of the videocassettes, which in 2000 ran as long as 19 minutes, gives campaigns the unique ability to fully flesh out who candidates are and what they stand for. What do the campaigns choose to do with that extra time? How heavily do presidential campaigns rely on polls and focus groups to determine the content found in their candidate videocassette? How do the campaigns frame their candidate? What images and issues are featured most prominently? Why do the campaigns choose to use certain images and issues? Are videocassette ads primarily issue-based ads or merely image-based biographical sketches? Answering this question can add another perspective to one of the more widely researched areas of political communication, that dealing with the image or issue orientation of TV spot ads.

What function does videocassette advertising serve in a primary campaign? Presidential campaigns spend valuable campaign time and money producing and distributing videocassette advertising. Why? What utility does it have for the campaigns? How heavily do campaigns use their candidate videocassette in their fund-raising activities? How successful are presidential campaigns at using their candidate video to generate "free media" coverage by the press? Another key question deals with what types of voters are targeted to receive candidate videocassettes. While voters in states such as Iowa and New Hampshire certainly top the list, other states must also be considered vital for video distribution. Do campaigns target the videos only to the party faithful or do they reach out to independents in the key primary and caucus states? Do the videocassettes serve different functions for each campaign? Has the function videocassette advertising serves changed over time? Do the frames, images, issues, and overall messages in the videocassettes define the candidate or the voters the candidate is attempting to win over?

How are presidential primary campaign videocassettes different from their closest political cousin, the presidential campaign film? There are distinct differences between presidential campaign films (which are shown to a mass audience during the general election campaign) and presidential primary videos (which are strategically targeted during the early months of the primaries), but there are key similarities (Morreale, 1994a, 1994b, 1993, 1991; Novak, 1997, 1995; Timmerman, 1996). Both run far longer than TV spots, providing the extra time needed to flesh out the images, issues and symbolic roles of the candidates. Indeed, the campaign film is the longest produced ad spot that a presidential candidate runs during the general election campaign, and the primary video is the longest produced ad spot that a presidential challenger runs during the primary phase of the campaign. This extra length of time gives campaigns the best opportunity to make their case and connect with voters thus, analyzing campaign films and primary videos provides for a useful exploration of political advertising.

While presidential incumbents and challengers have used campaign films, which can run 10 to 15 minutes in length, to present themselves and their issues to voters since the 1920s, Ronald Reagan's 1984 re-election film, "A New Beginning," began the modern era of the genre (Morreale, 1993). Reagan's campaign team used parts of his film in TV spots, and they ran a longer, repackaged version of the film as a 30-minute commercial late in the campaign on ABC, CBS, NBC, WTBS, CBN, and ESPN. In the end, millions of people watched the film (Morreale, 1991, p. 9). Part of understanding the function of presidential primary videos will come from exploring how the videos differ from and are similar to general election campaign films.

These and other questions are answered by examining the primary campaign videos of the six Democratic and Republican presidential candidates—conservative activist Gary Bauer, former senator Bill Bradley, Texas governor George W. Bush, magazine publisher Steve Forbes, Vice President Al Gore, and Senator John McCain—who released presidential primary "meet the candidate videos" during the 2000 presidential primary.

A number of methods are used in exploring the videos of the 2000 presidential primary candidates. Frame analysis of the primary campaign videos reveals what story lines political campaigns used in presenting their candidates to voters and the media. A quantitative content analysis lists and rank orders the candidate videos' issues and images to gain insight into how the videos package candidates. Finally, in-depth interviews with producers of candidate videocassettes confirms findings discovered through frame analysis and content analysis and also leads research about primary campaign videos into new directions.

Employing several methods to aid understanding—often called "triangulation"—has a distinguished history (Lincoln and Guba, 1985; Denzin, 1988; Lindlof, 1995). Webb et al. (1966, p. 3) argues that the triangulation of methods can make a research design more valid: "Once a proposition has been confirmed by two or more measurement processes, the uncertainty of its interpretation is greatly reduced. The most persuasive evidence comes through a triangulation of measurement process. If a proposition can survive the onslaught of a series of imperfect measures, with all their imperfect error, confidence should be placed in it." The present study goes beyond merely using several methods. Rather, the study discovers meaning in the 2000 presidential primary videos by drawing inferences found in the many methods. This tactic is encouraged by many scholars. As Dreher (1994) notes: "In those countless studies that combine quantitative and qualitative techniques in a triangulated design, only rarely is an attempt made to integrate the two components of the study. Rather they are treated like two separate studies in one project. This treatment is unfortunate because even a simple comparison of the results of the two components could lend confirmation to and thus strengthen the argument" (p. 289).

Each method being used in the present study was selected because it helps answer the main research questions in a unique way, and—most importantly—the combination of these particular methods should provide a recursive understanding of the function of presidential primary videos. In other words, just like the dots of an Impressionist painting, no one dot tells you anything; it is only when many dots combine that a larger, meaningful vision emerges.

For example, quantitative content analysis can provide a consistent, valid coding scheme that includes operational definitions for phenomena being explored, such as the symbolic roles found in the videos. But while the findings from this method should answer part of the main research questions, additional methods could add so much more. The reason for this is that the operational definitions found in a manifest content analysis demand, as Pauly (1991) puts it, "consistency of denotation and absence of connotation. The language of everyday life, however, is lushly metaphorical, wildly contradictory, willfully connotative, and cynically strategic. What can researchers hope to know of human communication if their methods ban the play of meanings?" (p. 6). Frame analysis can add meaning to the operational definitions by showing what dominant story lines are present in the various videos.

But these data, too, only tell part of the story. In-depth interviews with the producers of these videos can reveal what frames the campaigns thought they were using, what symbolic roles they were trying to convey to voters, and what function their video had in their campaign strategy.

Despite the multiple methods, framing theory will be the unifying theory for this study. In addition to frame analysis, framing theory has been used in content analysis (Iyengar, 1991) and in-depth interviews (Gitlin, 1980). This unifying theory is designed to bind together the several methods used in the study to help discover the functions of presidential primary campaign videos.

Throughout the analysis of the videocassettes, framing theory is used to understand how the videos package the candidates. According to Entman (1993): "Framing essentially involves selection and salience. To frame is to select some aspects of a perceived reality and make them more salient in a communicating text, in such a way as to promote a particular problem definition, causal interpretation, moral evaluation, and/or treatment recommendation for the item described" (p. 52). Gamson and Modigliani (1987) defined a frame as a "central organizing idea or story line that provides meaning to an unfolding strip of events" (p. 143). This story line, which includes visual and verbal elements, is constructed by "symbol handlers" (Gitlin, 1980, p. 7), who may be journalists, elites, interest groups, or political advertisers.

Framing in political communication has been used mostly to understand what story lines journalists use in presenting news on political issues and activists (Ashley and Olson, 1998; Gamson, 1992; Gitlin, 1980; Iyengar, 1991; Pan and Kosicki, 1993). Framing research on how advertisers frame their products is just beginning to emerge. Morreale (1991) used a textual frame analysis to explore the verbal and visual techniques used in Ronald Reagan's 1984 general election campaign film. She argued that "the Republicans used framing to create a 'reality'" (p. 96) through the use of ideological, mythic and rebirth frames in the film. She also noted the utility of framing theory with regard to exploring this type of political advertising (pp. 6, 97).

So framing theory holds that humans (whether they be private individuals, journalists, interest groups, or advertisers) create story lines to organize large amounts of information into an efficient package for audiences to interpret. Seen from this perspective, framing allows political advertisers to organize large amounts of biographical and issue-oriented information about their candidate into an efficient package for audiences to interpret.

AN ORIGINAL CONTRIBUTION TO POLITICAL COMMUNICATION

This study builds on the existing general knowledge of presidential communication, political advertising, primary campaign strategies and direct marketing techniques. Further, it provides an original contribution to political communication research by adding knowledge about what function presidential primary videos serve in presidential primary campaigns. These videos, their messages, and their function have been virtually ignored by current political communication scholarship.

While much scholarship on presidential campaigning examines general election activity, less is known about primary campaign communication, which includes presidential primary campaign videocassettes. At the general election level, research has been done on a wide variety of political communication media, including 30- to 60-second TV ads (Johnson-

Cartee and Copeland, 1997; West, 1997; Jamieson, 1996; Diamond and Bates, 1992; and Kern, 1989).

Political communication scholarship on presidential primary campaign activities is harder to find. Existing research indicates that primary campaign communication can have powerful effects. Research on TV spot ads shows that campaign advertising can exercise influence on voters' perception of the candidates during primary campaigning (Pfau et al., 1995). Furthermore, presidential candidates who advertised early and retain a fixed image fare well in comparison with candidates who produce multiple images (Devlin, 1994). Other research focuses on how voters gather political information before they vote (Lowden et al., 1994) and on the effects of and relationship between "issue" and "image" presidential TV spots in primary campaigning (Shyles, 1984).

Primary ads tend to be targeted to key voters in selected battleground states and attempt to make personal and political distinctions among the many candidates in the race (Kendall, 2000). Kendall further argues the following: "Advertising in the primaries has the potential to be more influential than advertising in the general election, particularly in the early primaries, because of the relatively unformed views of the public, as well as the fact that many candidates are not well known" (p. 92). Other research looks at the changing nature of presidential nominating contests and the increased significance of primaries. Bartels (1988) found in today's primary-dominated nominating contests the winners often get decided very early in the primary season and that momentum is an essential ingredient of the winning candidates' strategy. Bartels notes that while general election outcomes are "relatively uncomplicated" and "can be predicted in advance with considerable accuracy," primaries are different:

The process by which each party chooses its candidate for the presidency presents quite another picture. Instead of two contenders there may be half a dozen or more. Some candidates may be well-known political figures; others may be virtually unknown to the electorate. The issues dividing them may have little to do with the issues on which the winner will eventually wage the general election campaign. And they compete in fifty separate state-level delegate selection processes governed by a bizarre assortment of complex rules. (p. 5)

Researching presidential primary communication is significant because today it is primaries, not the traditional national nominating conventions, that select a presidential nominee. West (1997) found that from the 1920s to the 1960s, only about 40% of convention delegates were selected by primaries; the rest were hand picked by party leaders. But since 1968, about 70% of delegates get picked through primaries (p. 11). This shift occurred due to nomination reform movements instigated in the 1970s (Bartels, 1988, pp. 17–24). Bartels summarized the changing significance of presidential primaries:

The new system is dominated by candidates and by the news media; the old system was dominated by professional party politicians. The central decision-making mechanism in the new system is mass voting; the central mechanism in the old system was face-to-face bargaining. The locus of choice in the new system is the primary ballot box; the locus of choice in the old system was the convention backroom. Every important feature of the contemporary nominating process was far less prominent in the process that gave us Franklin D. Roosevelt, Dwight D. Eisenhower, and (lest we forget) John W. Davis and Warren G. Harding. (p. 13)

It is in this "new system" of selecting a presidential nominee that primary campaign videocassettes make sense for the candidates. The biographical and issue information provided in these videos helps candidates cross what Bartels contends is the candidates' first hurdle in gaining the nomination: establishing "familiarity" with voters (p. 57). By being mailed to the homes of potential primary voters, the videos target the audience most likely to decide their electoral fate. Furthermore, as Roberts (1979, 1981) found, the impression voters have about candidates forms quite early during a campaign, and these impressions are aided by information disseminated through the media.

Mass communication and political science research indicates that presidential candidates cannot rely on the media to carry their message to primary voters. Media coverage by TV network newscasts during primaries has been shown to focus more on the "horse race" aspect of campaigning and less on explaining the specific issues the candidates are talking about (Speckman, 1999; Bartels, 1988). In addition, the "newshole" that journalists need to fill for each publication or broadcast tends to get smaller and smaller for presidential primary campaign news as the primary season progresses (Robinson and Sheehan, 1983). Presidential primary videocassettes represent a way to counteract the sparse "free media" attention provided during the campaign with a positive "paid media" message targeted to the voters who matter the most.

Political communication research on direct marketing techniques, which includes direct mail and videos, explores the topic broadly and mostly overlooks presidential primary campaign videos (Denton and Woodward, 1998; Colford, 1994; Tait, 1994; Luntz, 1988; Reynolds, 1989). Still, when talking about direct mail videos in a general sense, Trent and Friedenberg (1995, p. 272) argue that there are "enormous advantages" in direct marketing's ability to "target an audience more precisely than virtually any other form of advertising."

Direct marketing of candidate videos has become widespread because of improved technology, economies of scale, and response rate success. Trent and Friedenberg (1995) note that: "According to some studies, as many as 40% of those who receive an unsolicited video will watch it, a far higher rate than unsolicited mail typically generates. Moreover, studies suggest that the response rates, whether the video is simply seeking voter support or seeking volunteers and/or money, typically runs 20% higher than direct mail" (p. 282).

Political communication scholars and political scientists have tried to understand the use and effects of political advertising, marketing and the media in presidential primary campaigns. But while TV spot advertising research is abundant, scholarship on presidential primary campaign videocassettes provides merely a brief history of this unique type of advertising.

DEFINITION OF PRESIDENTIAL PRIMARY VIDEOS

Some presidential candidates have other videos in addition to—or instead of—a "meet the candidate video." Al Gore, with the aid of union cooperation, distributed an 11-minute videocassette to union members that included a 6-minute biography of Gore and a 5-minute segment titled "Al Gore Speaks to America's Working Families." More than 25,000 union households in Iowa and New Hampshire received the video, which included AFL-CIO union leader John Sweeny's endorsement of Gore (Magleby, 2000). This video is in addition to the 10-minute video Gore's campaign mass mailed to voters and put up on the Gore presidential web site.

In the months preceding George W. Bush's official presidential announcement—and distribution of his official 13-minute "meet the candidate" video—the Texas governor sent out videos to potential donors highlighting what he had accomplished in Texas. Television ad spots from Bush's 1998 gubernatorial re-election campaign were mixed in with clips of media coverage of Bush's Texas record. The videotape noted that Bush had not announced his candidacy for president and acknowledged that the Texas governor may not choose to run for the White House.

Two other 2000 presidential candidates, Alan Keyes and Orrin Hatch, chose to forgo the traditional 5- to 20-minute "meet the candidate video," opting instead to sell or distribute longer-form videos (one lasting more than 2 hours) that were merely filmed speeches by the candidate. A third candidate, former Tennessee governor Lamar Alexander selectively mailed a video only to top contributors of his 1996 presidential run.

This study focuses on the "meet the candidate videos" for the presidential primary candidates who were successful enough to survive the early nomination contests in Iowa and New Hampshire. This decision was based on a desire to explore the rhetorical and visual themes used by the most serious candidates to introduce themselves—or in some cases reintroduce themselves—to the American people. The videos of Alexander, Hatch, and Keyes were excluded because their length and/or their one-dimensional approach place them outside the definition of the "meet the candidate videos."

Chapter Two

The Function Videocassette Campaigning Serves in Presidential Primaries

Some consultants already foresee a time when video players are standard home equipment and when videocassettes of a candidate giving his pitch are mass-produced and mailed to volunteers, contributors, and the general public.

Larry Sabato, *The Rise of Political Consultants*, 1981

Twenty years after Sabato's prophetic statement, candidate videocassette ads are everywhere. In the 2000 presidential race, all major party candidates who were significant enough to survive past the Iowa caucus and New Hampshire primary mailed videocassette ads to voters. The video ads, which were sent out in summer 1999, ran between 5 and 19 minutes and included biographical and issue segments. During the last weeks of the general election, Vice President Al Gore fought slumping poll numbers against Texas governor George W. Bush by distributing thousands of copies of a 10-minute video that critiqued Bush's record on health care, education, and the environment. Democratic volunteers who knocked on doors before election day carried the video with them and offered to show it to voters (Meckler, 2000).

In addition to presidential hopefuls, candidates for other offices also take advantage of videocassette ads. Hillary Clinton kicked off her U.S. Senate bid in February 2000 by screening her "meet the candidate" video to members of the press. Titled "Hillary," the 15-minute videocassette was produced by Linda Bloodworth-Thomason, who created Bill Clinton's 1992 and 1996 presidential campaign films. Copies of the videocassette also were distributed to six hundred smaller gatherings of her supporters throughout New York state (Marks, 2000).

With the omnipresence of candidate videocassettes today, it might be hard to remember that the technology to do all this is only one generation old. Videocassette recorders (VCRs) were first marketed for home use in the mid-1970s. The machines cost between $700 and $1,500 apiece, and partly because of the price, just 2% of U.S. households had a VCR by 1980 (Cobb, 1980; Krugman, Shamp, and Johnson, 1991).

The story of the emergence of videocassette advertising in presidential campaigns is one that speaks to the revolutionary changes in the technological, cultural, and political environments over the past 20 years. Three key changes facilitated its emergence and widespread use: the increase in VCR penetration, the decreases in cost of VCR technology, and the decreasing effectiveness of traditional political advertising.

Advertising historians such as Donald Avery (1991) view the "media in general and advertising in particular as mirrors of society, on the one hand influencing culture and society and on the other being influenced and shaped by those same variables." Roland Marchand (1985) in *Advertising the American Dream* argued that advertising should be studied as "reflections of American culture." Presidential primary campaign videocassettes certainly can be explored in this way. The changes that sparked the growth of candidate videocassettes are quite stark:

The increase in VCR penetration. While just 2% of U.S. households had a VCR by 1980 and just 20% had one by 1984, in 1988 VCR penetration exceeded 50% of the country (Grove, 1987). Videocassette campaigning didn't become widespread until 1988, by which time VCR penetration had become widespread. By 2000 more than 90% of households were projected to have a VCR (Trent and Friedenberg, 1995).

The decrease in cost of direct mail videos. Producing, duplicating, and mailing videocassettes was prohibitively expensive for most candidates during the late 1970s and early 1980s. By 1988, the cost to produce and deliver videocassettes was about $5 per video (Sabato and Beiler, 1988). At this point, a majority of the Democratic and Republican presidential candidates included videocassettes in their advertising strategy (Grove, 1987). By 1992, it cost just $1.25 per video (Koeppel, 1992). In 2000, the cost got as low as $1.10 per video (Kranish, 1999). Because most campaigns have limited financial resources, the decrease in cost has made videocassette advertising a more cost-effective weapon in their arsenals. In 1988, for example, while most campaigns had these videos, most campaigns distributed only small numbers of them. Arizona governor Bruce Babbitt sent out 500 videos during his campaign (Milne, 1987). In contrast, Arizona senator John McCain's 2000 campaign mailed more than 50,000 videos (Kranish, 1999).

The decrease in the effectiveness of traditional political advertising. Evidence has been mounting that traditional political advertising, such as 30-second

TV spot ads, has become less cost-effective since the 1980s. Candidates have found it increasingly difficult to reach the audiences they need (Glasser, 2000; Walter, 1999). Cable TV has splintered the market, providing 50 to 100 stations to viewers in cities where there once were only 4 or 5 stations. Neal Oxman of the Campaign Group Inc., a Philadelphia media consulting firm, argues that traditional TV spot ads have been losing their effectiveness for some time. "Local TV stations charge 5 to 10 times what they did 20 years ago to deliver the same audience, " he says. "They're getting away with flat-out stealing compared to what they're delivering" (Morgan, 2000). According to Jim Jordon, political director of the Democratic Senatorial Campaign Committee: "Even the media guys will say, the influence of conventional television advertising is waning. There's just less bang for the buck from TV.... It's an irony. We're spending more even as there's an awareness that it's less effective" (Glasser, 2000).

Increasingly, candidates at all levels are turning to alternative campaign advertising to deliver the audience neglected by network and cable television. Nonbroadcast video, which includes presidential primary videos, has filled the need, not only for presidential candidates, but for candidates for offices from state representative to sheriff. There are four key advantages to nonbroadcast video: viewership, information density, targetablility, and cost effectiveness (Walter, 2000, pp. 196–198).

Loyal viewership. Walter notes that viewers of these videos focus on the message of the ad more than on "the distracting visual environments of most other media. Once the viewer hits the 'play' button, he or she is engaged; there are no other channels to surf or pages to turn" (p. 197). Other research, such as that from Krugman (1985), supports the argument that VCR viewing is done with more active participation than with traditional television.

Increased information density. Not only do videocassette ads have more time than TV spot ads to send out a message, viewers also have the opportunity to replay the video as many times as they wish at no added cost to the campaign.

Increased targetablility. "Television ads, even when run on narrow-niche cable stations, may still reach tens of thousands of people for whom the information may have no connection or relevance," Walter argues. But videocassette advertising:

is specifically designed to address a limited group of people: blue-collar union women; homeowners who pay more than $3,000 a year in property taxes; retired Jewish senior citizens; rural evangelicals; suburban, professional African Americans; or the residents of a city with a prohibitively expensive television market. Once the audience is identified by mailing lists, the message, the information, everything [it] says and shows can be designed to attract their attention, stimulate their interest, and, it is hoped, persuade them to support the cause or the candidate. (p. 197)

Walter's comment about the ability of videocassette ads to efficiently reach "the residents of a city with a prohibitively expensive television market" holds special importance for the study of presidential primary videos. These videocassettes, which are mailed out during the early months of the primary campaign, are targeted to influence voters in key states such as Iowa and New Hampshire.

Past political communication research has found that buying TV ad time in New Hampshire, especially, can be prohibitively expensive because to effectively cover the state, ad time needs to be bought in multiple TV markets, including Portland, Maine; Burlington, Vermont; and Manchester, New Hampshire. In addition, even though Massachusetts residents can't vote in the New Hampshire primary, the expensive Boston market also has to be included in a candidate's ad budget because the city's stations have approximately 17% New Hampshire viewers (Devlin, 1994; p. 82). This inefficient use of political advertising dollars on TV spot ads is a key reason why direct-mailed videocassettes make so much sense for presidential candidates at the primary level.

Cost effectiveness. This is perhaps the most compelling advantage videocassette ads have over traditional TV spot ads. While a 5-minute videocassette currently can be targeted to 20,000 households for approximately $50,000, according to Walter, "only a handful of network television markets in the country would require less than $50,000 to achieve a reach and frequency to rival a 5-minute [videocassette ad]" (p. 198).

THE BEGINNINGS OF VIDEOCASSETTE CAMPAIGNING

While VCRs entered into home use during the 1970s, early videocassette technology goes back to the 1950s. In 1956 the Ampex Corporation marketed videotape machines to television broadcasters, allowing the stations to record TV shows to be broadcast later. By 1969 the Sony Corporation began creating an affordable VCR for households. Throughout the 1970s, two VCR formats—Betamax and VHS—vied for market dominance. The VHS format eventually won out and reached into hundreds of millions of homes (Lardner, 1987; Consumer Electronics Association, 2000).

VCRs began to capture the public's imagination during the 1980s, and a new industry cropped up to meet the growing consumer demand for videocassettes. One of these new companies, Blockbuster, opened its first video store in Dallas in 1985. Within five years, the company had 1,500 stores (Levy, 1989; Blockbuster, 2000).

By the mid-1980s, videocassette campaigning had begun to emerge as a viable advertising strategy for most candidates. *The Washington Post* (Video production group forms local chapter, 1985) noted that the growing use of videocassettes by politicians, corporations, and trade associations had created a $10-million-a-year industry that was "virtually nonexistent 10 years ago." The paper dubbed the nation's capital's new videotaping industry a "sleeping giant" (p. F21).

The 1980 presidential election marked the first time presidential hopefuls tested the public's familiarity with VCRs and used videocassettes to get their messages across to voters. The 1980 campaign of former Texas congressman and United Nations ambassador George Bush is credited with being the first at the presidential level to employ videocassette advertising (Sabato and Beiler, 1988). The campaign used Bush's videocassette mainly as a fund-raising tool, showing it to groups of supporters who gathered in living rooms in key primary and caucus states (p. 8). It wasn't until 1988, however, that increases in VCR penetration and the affordability of VCR technology made videocassette campaigning feasible for most presidential hopefuls.

Another reason videocassette campaigning was slow to gain acceptance was that it forced campaigns to change the way they organized themselves, according to Tom Edmonds, who has produced political videocassettes for interest groups and presidential candidates since the mid-1980s:

Trying to get this to happen was difficult because it crossed over more than one discipline. For instance, the media guy ... knew how to do the radio and TV, but he didn't produce videos. The direct mail guy knew how to put ink on paper but he had no experience with sending the videos out.... The fund-raising people the same thing. They knew how to raise money, and they knew how to raise money with mail, but they didn't know how to raise money with videos.... The media guy had to produce this thing that the fund-raiser guy could use, or the direct mail guy had to work with the video guy. And oftentimes they weren't even in the same damn meeting. You know, other than, "What does the logo look like?" they had no reason to even acknowledge each other's existence. And so there were a lot of problems. Nobody would recommend it because it balked at their normal way of doing business. It was not a tool that people had in their toolbox. (Interview with the author on January 3, 2001)

1988: VIDEOCASSETTE CAMPAIGNING BECOMES WIDESPREAD

By the 1988 presidential primaries, a majority of the major party candidates—11 out of 13—employed videocassette advertising. The candidates on the Democratic side were Massachusetts governor Michael Dukakis, Missouri congressman Richard Gephardt, Illinois senator Paul Simon, the Reverend Jesse Jackson, Tennessee senator Al Gore, Arizona governor Bruce Babbitt, and former Colorado senator Gary Hart. The GOP field included Vice President George Bush, Kansas senator Bob Dole, New York congressman Jack Kemp, Delaware governor Pete Du Pont, the Reverend Pat Robertson, and former secretary of state Alexander Haig.

With so many hats in the ring, the 1988 primary exacerbated many of the growing problems with traditional TV advertising. TV air time in early battleground states such as Iowa and New Hampshire became flooded with candidate commercials. David Zamichow, general manager of WMUR-TV in New Hampshire, told *The Manchester Union Leader* in 1988 that the glut of presidential commercials prevented him from spacing them out over the broadcast day and forced him to run three or more political ads in a row (Fahey, 1988). This unusual practice had the effect of jumbling the messages the candidates were trying to get across to voters and blurring the lines between the candidates.

Muddying the political waters is especially troubling for candidates in a primary campaign because, as Pfau et al. (1993) argue, primaries "constitute intra-party contests, thus virtually erasing the impact of political party identification on candidate preference" (p. 275). In addition, the short life span of primaries forces voters to learn about candidates in a short period of time. "This places a premium on quickly absorbed personal and issue cues," according to Popkin (1991, p. 223). Political communication research shows that without the strong pull of party partisanship, campaign communication in primaries takes on an enhanced power to influence voter perceptions of the candidates (Becker and McCombs, 1978; Kennamer, 1990).

Not surprisingly, the 1988 candidates increased their efforts to use new communication technology to target their message and set themselves apart from the pack. Videocassette campaigning allowed candidates to present a far longer message than they could in a 30-second spot. This type of advertising also could be finely targeted to various groups. One voting block, organized labor, invited presidential candidates from both parties to videotape 4-minute campaign messages, which were then compiled and shown in thousands of union halls across America. The 66-minute videocassette was titled "Democracy at Work." Paul Taylor (1987), a reporter for *The Washington Post*, sat in on one of these union hall video screenings, which featured speeches from 13 presidential hopefuls. Taylor found the blue-collar audience surprisingly receptive to the medium. The crowd watched intently, sometimes agreeing with comments made by the candidates and sometimes making a joke at the candidates' expense. Taylor wrote: "The reactions are a reminder that American voters, first and foremost, are video-literate. They may take their time to reach judgment about a candidate's policies and character. But on everything from ear lobes to body language, they're quick studies."

The videocassettes that each presidential candidate produced and mailed to voters also took advantage of the growing consumer familiarity with VCRs and videotape. Lloyd Grove (1987) of *The Washington Post* chronicled how videocassette advertising began to change how primary campaigns were run: "Among the new and acceptable political pastimes in Iowa and New Hampshire are the video coffee klatsch, the video house party, even the video fund-raiser."

Of the 11 Democratic and Republican candidates who produced and distributed candidate videocassettes, the basic format of the videos was relatively similar: start out with a personal and political biography of the candidate, then include a segment where the candidate talks about key issues of the day. Bob Dole's primary videocassette, titled "To the Stars Through Difficulties," followed this format. The 18-minute video traces Dole's humble beginnings in Russell, Kansas, then recounts how Dole overcame crippling injuries suffered during World War II. Dole's close relationship with his second wife, former Secretary of Transportation Elizabeth Dole, also features prominently in the video, though his daughter and first wife receive no mention. Dole's political biography includes footage from a 1976 political rally when President Gerald Ford campaigned for re-election with then-vice presidential nominee Dole. The tape closes with Dole giving a campaign speech in front of a cornfield. Validation of the candidate comes from several sources, including Idaho senator Steven Symms. "Who's tough? The answer is Bob Dole. He's got a backbone of steel," Symms says (Hagstrom and Guskind, 1988).

Jack Kemp's videocassette is similar to Dole's in that it is divided into biographical and issue segments. This combination of image and issue appeals provided for a more comprehensive introduction of the candidate. The eight-minute video tells the story of Kemp's fabled professional football career as quarterback of the San Diego Chargers and the Buffalo Bills. The video transitions from personal biography to political biography and then to a discussion of issues. "Since he has left the football field, Jack has had even greater success," the narrator says. Kemp's service as a congressman from New York is detailed, as is his unwavering support for tax cuts. The video notes that "Jack Kemp persuaded Ronald Reagan to cut taxes" in the early 1980s and later "rushed to the White House and persuaded President Reagan to abandon" a plan to freeze Social Security benefits. The video ends with Kemp making a political speech. Validation of Kemp is provided by New Hampshire congressman Bob Smith, who introduces the video, and by media sources. The video notes that "*Time* magazine said Jack Kemp 'sold Reaganomics to Reagan'" (Blumenthal, 1987).

Dole's videocassette cost $30,000 to produce, which was about as much as most campaigns were willing to spend that year on this new advertising instrument (Grove, 1987). Most candidate videos were distributed in the summer and fall of 1987 to establish an initial, positive tone for the campaign. Dole's video, which debuted the week before his November 9, 1987, formal presidential announcement speech, was shown at approximately 1,300 political house parties in key primary and caucus states (Grove, 1987). Mari Maseng, Dole's press secretary, told Grove the videocassette was a good surrogate speaker for the senator, saying it was "the next best thing to having Bob Dole in their living room" (p. A7).

Many candidates used their videocassettes as surrogate speakers. David Axelrod, who produced Paul Simon's videocassette, told Grove that Simon's video allowed the campaign to reach more voters. "On any given day, there are hundreds of places a candidate would like to be but can't be," he said. "The video affords the candidate a chance to be in all those places at once" (p. A7).

Simon's six-minute video provided a biographical introduction to the candidate, chronicling Simon's beginnings as a crusading journalist and publisher. Simon's wife and other family members give testimonials about the senator. Toward the end of the video, Simon talks about issues, including the Iran-Contra Affair, during a campaign speech (Simon, 1987).

Some campaigns also used videocassette advertising as a fund-raising instrument. Pat Robertson, who won a surprise second place in Iowa, sold "video volunteer kits" for $19.88 apiece. The campaign claimed to have sold thousands of the kits (Grove, 1987). Volunteers who bought the kit got a videocassette that tried to make the religious broadcaster look "presidential."

Robertson's 27-minute video, titled "Pat Robertson: Who Is This Man," includes a parental advisory due to certain graphic material and addresses such issues as abortion, family values, and U.S. involvement in Central America. The video's image-based moments include footage of a Robertson campaign rally, with strobe lights flashing and the national anthem playing. Imagery includes the American flag, the Statue of Liberty, and fireworks. Robertson then is shown emerging from darkness to speak to the cheering crowd (Robertson, 1987; Hagstrom and Guskind, 1988).

The image and issue appeals presented in the videocassettes often were designed to help inoculate the candidate and change existing perceptions of the campaign. Bruce Babbitt created his videocassettes in the fall of 1987 to respond to criticism that the candidate's lackluster debate appearances that summer showed that he lacked, as Babbitt's New Hampshire state director Mike Muir put it, "television capabilities" (Grove, 1987). So Babbitt's video, which was targeted to about five hundred uncommitted Democratic activists in New Hampshire, included footage of Babbitt giving positive debate performances (p. A7). Kemp's videocassette, which began being distributed in July 1987 to allow the candidate a head start on wooing voters, also served an inoculation function. Paul Young, Kemp's campaign director in the Granite State, told Laura Kiernan, of *The Boston Globe*, that the video allowed the candidate to be seen more favorably as a campaigner. Kemp had been criticized during the race for being too long-winded in his speech-making. Young noted that with the videocassette, "It will be the first time anybody walks away from Jack Kemp wanting more."

Dukakis's campaign, which produced a candidate videocassette that followed roughly the same biographical structure as the videos for the other candidates, received more attention for the second video it produced, one that was distributed to the press and attacked rival candidate Delaware senator Joseph Biden. The video, which implied that Biden plagiarized parts of his political stump speeches, led to the senator's early withdrawal from the race (Vennochi, 1987; Grove 1987; Hagstrom and Guskind, 1988).

1992: CANDIDATE VIDEOCASSETTES HELP CREATE A FRONT-RUNNER

In 1992, the use of presidential primary campaign videocassettes assisted in weeding out one White House hopeful and propelling another to national recognition. During the early days of the New Hampshire race, Virginia governor Douglas Wilder's campaign team put together a videocassette that stressed a "New Democrat" image and targeted the video's message to the state's Democrats and Independents. The video touted Wilder's medal-winning Korean War experience and his budget-balancing fiscal conservatism (Page, 1993). The campaign then screened Wilder's videocassette for four focus groups in New Hampshire to get a feel for what chances the Virginia governor would have in the Granite State.

After the focus groups responded to the videocassette presentation, Wilder dropped out of the presidential race. Syndicated columnist Clarence Page, who later wrote about the experience, noted that the members of the New Hampshire focus groups were pleasantly disposed toward Wilder's biography and record on the issues, but when the videocassette was played, "their mood noticeably changed from joy to chagrin. In one eyebrow-raising outburst, a surprised woman told the woman sitting next to her: 'He's black!' It wasn't that they were antiblack, they said. Rather, 'My neighbors probably wouldn't like it' or 'I don't think New Hampshire will go for that.'

Another self-proclaimed "New Democrat," Arkansas governor Bill Clinton, found more success with his videocassette. Even before the official caucuses and primaries were held, Clinton's campaign mailed his videocassette, titled "The New Covenant," to delegates of the Florida Democratic Party's annual convention, which was held in December 1991. The high point of the convention was a straw poll where the delegates voted their choice for president. Clinton's team hoped that a win, even in an unofficial straw poll, would help garner national attention in the weeks before the crucial contests in Iowa and New Hampshire. Clinton won the Florida straw poll by 54%. Thomas Rosenstiel (1992) of *The Los Angeles Times* wrote that Clinton's Florida victory "helped make him the party's nominal front-runner, and, in turn, the leader in fund-raising." Rosenstiel placed much of the credit for Clinton's win on his strategic use of video-cassette campaigning: "To win that straw poll, Clinton's campaign sent out a 16-minute video to all 2,000 delegates at the Florida convention. Approximately 1,000 who were undecided or leaning toward Clinton got extra attention: Messengers delivered a video to their homes, along with a letter from the candidate." Frank Greer, Clinton's media consultant, told Rosenstiel that videocassette campaigning was ideal for the front-loaded 1992 presidential primary: "With the short campaign we are in, they are more important this year than ever" (p. 5).

The Clinton videocassette frames him as a change for the party and for America. The first lines spoken in the video reinforce this image: "This election is about change: change in our party, change in our leadership, change in our nation." The videocassette, which is similar in structure to most previous candidate videos in that it combines biographical and issue information, is also part motivational speech to the party faithful and part political diatribe. The video's biographical segment includes footage of Clinton's famous Boy's Nation handshake with President Kennedy in 1963. A male narrator touts Clinton's political accomplishments: Rhodes Scholar, longest serving sitting governor, "and this year he was voted most effective in the nation by his fellow governors, both Democrat and Republican"(Clinton, 1991).

About one-third of the video includes attacks on the incumbent president. In making his points, Clinton uses some of the 1988 campaign rhetoric of George Bush—the concept of a "thousand points of light"—to attack President Bush's performance in office: "I can tell you, my friends, when there is no national vision, no national leadership, no national direction, a thousand points of light leaves a lot of darkness."

The last third of the video focuses on Clinton's issue appeals. He talks about health care reform, education policy, and he calls for a national service plan. Other segments of the video address "economic growth" and "restoring the American dream." Clinton talks about welfare reform, business competitiveness, and the need for the wealthy to pay their fair share in taxes. Clinton's video, which served as a fund-raising tool, contains a call to action at the end that includes an Arkansas phone number and post office box to contribute money and/or volunteer (Clinton, 1991).

Media validation of Clinton's record, vision, and political viability are used heavily in his video. Positive quotes about Clinton from articles in *Time* magazine, *The Washington Post, New York* magazine, and *The Philadelphia Inquirer* are shown on the screen and narrated to the viewer at the same time. A quote from the *Inquirer* (October 6, 1991 issue) calls Clinton "The Moderate Radical." Joe Klein, who would later be the "anonymous" writer of *Primary Colors,* is quoted in a *New York* magazine article noting that "the Arkansas governor's New Covenant [the slogan for Clinton's policy initiatives as well as the title for his candidate videocassette] puts all the pieces together."

Other Democratic presidential candidates who used videocassette advertising in 1992, including Iowa senator Tom Harkin and Nebraska senator Bob Kerrey, found more modest success with their videos. Harkin's videocassette, which was sent to voters in Iowa, New Hampshire, and Southern states, was criticized for being short on policy specifics (Koeppel, 1992; Rosenstiel, 1992). The video traces Harkin's childhood in poverty as the son of a coal miner and touts his 23-year marriage (Rosenstiel, 1992).

Kerrey's videocassette, which, like Governor Wilder's video, was shown to focus groups to measure voter interest in the candidate, also focused heavily on the candidate's biography. The video, titled "Nebraska at Its Best: Bob Kerrey, A Personal Profile," recounts Kerrey's Vietnam War heroics, including how he won the Medal of Honor after losing part of his right leg during combat. Unlike the videos for Clinton and Harkin, Kerrey's videocassette was not produced solely for his presidential run. The video was originally made for his 1988 senatorial campaign and additional footage of his victory speech that year was then included in the 1992 version.

The most emotionally charged moment in the video comes during Kerrey's Senate victory celebration when he sings to a silent crowd of his supporters an Australian antiwar ballad, "And the band played 'Waltzing Matilda,'" that bears a haunting similarity to his own war experience: "They collected the wounded, the legless, the maimed … and shipped us all back to Australia.…And the band played "Waltzing Matilda" as they carried us down the gangway. And nobody cheered; they just stood and stared and turned all their faces away" (Kerry, 1991).

Mike McCurry, who during the 1992 race was an advisor in Kerrey's campaign, told Rosenstiel that videocassette advertising was ideal for highly motivated primary voters. The videos are "especially effective for the politically literate who want to know how a candidate comes across on television," McCurry said.

By 1992, doubts about the effectiveness of videocassette campaigning had begun to melt away. Dan Koeppel of *Adweek's Marketing Week* interviewed one GOP political consultant who became a true believer of videocassettes after one of his clients used them in a run for a state office in Illinois: "The candidate used no other advertising, bought no TV time, no direct mail or telemarketing. Before the [videocassette] mailing, 70% of the electorate was undecided. After the mailing, 80% of those who received the cassette voted for the candidate.

Candidates at all levels—from races for governor to mayor—bought into videocassette advertising (Best, 1990; Lonetree, 1993). Driving these changes included the dramatic decrease in the price to produce and mail the videocassettes—$1.25 per video in 1992 as opposed to $5 in 1988—as well as the shrinking effectiveness of traditional TV ads. Low voter turnout rates and the increasing ease in voter targeting also were contributing factors. "Candidates will no longer even bother with mass TV buys in which more than half of the viewers simply won't be influenced by the ad," Koeppel wrote.

1996: "IF YOU LIVE IN IOWA OR NEW HAMPSHIRE, YOU CAN GET [A CANDIDATE VIDEOCASSETTE] FOR YOUR PET"

Four years after Bill Clinton vaulted to front-runner status after targeting his videocassette to voters in a Florida Democratic straw poll, GOP presidential contenders tried the same tactic with Florida Republicans. As with the 1991 Democratic straw poll, the 1995 GOP-sponsored straw poll was significant politically because it occurred weeks before Iowa and New Hampshire voted their choice for president. The Republican candidates attempted to sway the outcome of the Florida straw poll, which included 3,400 registered Republican delegates, by using a variety of retail political techniques—from giving Godiva chocolates to delegates to mailing them candidate videocassettes (Thompson and Kuhnhenn, 1995). Voters in early primary and caucus states also were saturated with candidate videocassettes. Mike Murphy, who was former Tennessee governor Lamar Alexander's media advisor and video producer, joked: "If you live in Iowa or New Hampshire, you can get one for your pet" (Feeney, 1996).

By 1996, nearly 80 percent of U.S. households with a television had a VCR (p. H8). Political campaigns were simply tapping into America's new video culture. Most Republican hopefuls for the 1996 race began mailing their videos in July and August 1995 to get a head start on reaching voters before the traditional barrage of 30-second TV ads began in earnest. Even campaigns that didn't last long, such as those of California governor Pete Wilson and automotive executive Morry Taylor, produced and distributed videocassette ads (Feeney, 1996).

One of the reasons videocassette ads continued to increase in popularity with campaigns was that so-called free media opportunities, such as coverage of candidates by the press, continued to dwindle. The average presidential candidate's TV network sound bite shrunk to an all-time low in 1996: 8.2 seconds, down from 9.8 seconds in 1988 (Lichter, Noyes and Kaid, 1997, p. 6). Network coverage of the presidential candidates also tended to be mostly negative in tone (pp. 8–10). Videocassette advertising represented a way to balance that negativity with a more positive image of the candidate.

The primary videocassettes of 1996 served many of the same functions as those from 1988 and 1992: surrogate introductory speaker early in the campaign, fund raiser, and vehicle for disseminating large amounts of image and issue information. Indiana senator Richard Lugar's nine-minute video, titled "Dick Lugar: Everything a President Should Be," was one that served a basic introductory function for voters, who knew almost nothing about the candidate (*The Manchester Union-Leader*, DiStaso, 1995). Lugar's campaign initially targeted the videos to New Hampshire residents who had a record of consistently voting. These regular voters were then telephoned by Lugar's staff and asked if they would like a copy of Lugar's video. Those who said "yes" got one in the mail. Lugar's campaign eventually sent out more than 50,000 videos (Feeney, 1996).

Like Lugar, Lamar Alexander distributed thousands of videocassette ads early in the race to introduce the little-known candidate (DiStaso, 1995). The 14-minute video was simply titled "Lamar!" and it highlighted Alexander's biography and stand on key issues. Alexander, wearing a plaid flannel shirt, later appears in the video to talk with voters. He pledges his support for school vouchers, a balanced budget amendment, welfare reform, and term limits for politicians. The plaid flannel color scheme, which was a trademark of Alexander's campaign, also is the color of the box that contains his videocassette (Alexander, 1995). This consistency helped maintain a unifying image of Alexander as a grass-roots candidate.

Texas senator Phil Gramm's campaign used his video to liven up the image of a man usually seen by voters on C-Span during the formalities of Senate hearings. Gramm's 16-minute video, titled "Gramm: Restoring the American Dream," shows him white-water rafting, fly-fishing, and shooting birds. The senator doesn't talk in specifics about issues, except to brag about his successful opposition to Clinton's failed health care overhaul plan (Gramm, 1995). The video, which was produced by Alex Castellanos, was sent to various states, as well as to every delegate of the Florida straw poll (Thompson and Kuhnhenn, 1995). Gramm's video differs from most primary videos in that it attacks a rival candidate, Dole. Gramm criticizes Dole's attempts to compromise with Clinton during the health care debate (Gramm: Restoring the American Dream, 1995).

Senate Majority Leader Bob Dole debuted his videocassette, titled "Bob Dole: An American Hero," in late September 1995 at a $250-a-head fund raiser, which drew 700 supporters. Dole's campaign eventually sent out more than 85,000 copies of his 14-minute primary video to various states. The video cost $60,000 to produce, plus $1.26 per tape, for a total campaign cost of $167,100 (Washington Notebook, 1995). Part of the video also played to about seven million viewers when an eight-minute version aired on the Denver-based TCI cable system as part of its free candidate coverage (Kurtz, 1995).

Like many other candidate videocassettes, Dole's used a single dominant story line to efficiently package the complex image and issue information contained within. For Dole, the small-town values frame connects his personal and political accomplishments. Wife Elizabeth Dole says he grew up in a small town in "a family that had a lot of love, but not much else." In talking about Dole's recovery from his World War II injuries, the narrator recounts Dole's lengthy exercise program to regain his strength and adds, "Bob Dole never gave up" (Dole, 1995).

Economic issues are addressed by Dole ("we can cut taxes and balance the budget" he tells a crowd) as he advocates giving more authority to state governments. Other domestic issues are outlined by Dole, while footage of farms, police officers, and children on bikes are seen. Footage outside the Supreme Court is seen alongside an audio of Dole's promise to appoint conservative judges. Foreign policy issues also are raised by Dole, while visuals are shown of the Iwo Jima Memorial and veterans at the Vietnam Memorial. Footage of President Reagan from March 1986 is shown as he tells a crowd, "Bob, from the heart, I thank you," for Dole's "principal role" in shepherding Reagan's tax overhaul plan through Congress.

Issue appeals in the video also play up Dole's values. In one scene, Dole is giving a speech attacking "gangsta" rap and the record companies that promote it. "It all comes down to values," Dole says. Humor and the warm relationship between the Doles also are displayed as values moments. "Why did I fall in love with Bob Dole? Well, it didn't hurt that he was the most handsome and strongest man I'd ever met, and probably the funniest," Elizabeth says in the video. Footage is then shown of Dole making jokes with David Letterman on the *Late Show with David Letterman* (Bob Dole: An American Hero, 1995).

Dole's videocassette received mixed reviews from the press (Barone, 1995; Kurtz, 1995; Mundy, 1995; Feeney, 1996). Alicia Mundy of *Mediaweek* was especially critical of the sometime somber tone in the video. "There's a big line between a makeover and embalming and Dole's media folks have crossed it, spit on it and stomped on it," she said.

CONCLUSIONS

Over the past 20 years several changes in the technological, cultural, and political environment fueled the emergence and growth of candidate videocassette advertising. Since 1980, America has evolved into a video culture, the cost of video equipment has become affordable, and political candidates have seen the benefits of alternative forms of advertising. By the 1988 presidential primary, videocassettes were a prerequisite for any serious presidential contender. By 1992, the videos began to influence the outcome of who received the presidential nomination.

What emerges as themes in the content of the videocassettes over the past 20 years is fairly consistent for both parties. The videos include a substantial mix of image and issue appeals, with biographical information being followed by the candidate talking about key issues of the day. Many videos included media validation to help the candidate appear presidential. While the videos were mostly positive, jabs at the opposition party are sometimes made, though intra-party attacks are almost nonexistent. The dominant story lines used in the videos to package the issue and image appeals also were similar among the candidates. Especially of note are the similarities between the videos of Clinton 1992 and Bush 2000, and between Gore 2000 and Dole 1996.

Presidential primary videos served several functions. The videos were employed as an instrument for basic candidate introduction, as a way to counter pre-existing perceptions of the candidate, and as a fund-raising tool. Most videocassettes were mailed to regular voters in Iowa and New Hampshire, while many candidates also targeted the videos to party activists in other states. Because the videos tended to be sent out early in the campaign season, the videos helped the candidates test the political waters, convincing some to continue and forcing others to drop out.

The emergence of videocassette campaigning didn't mean that candidates no longer sought the human touch to reach out to voters. Candidates still spent months in key primary states shaking hands and giving their traditional stump speeches. Some candidates who produced videocassette ads, such as Pete du Pont in 1988, personally spent as many as 60 days in Iowa and 80 days in New Hampshire (Koplinski, [2000], p. 248). Videocassette ads also didn't preclude the use of other alternative advertising strategies. Senator Paul Simon got humorous free media in 1988 when he appeared on NBC's "Saturday Night Live" with the singer Paul Simon (p. 545).

It remains to be seen how continuing technological changes will impact the future of videocassette advertising. These videos have worked in the past because so many voters have VCRs and are willing to use them. As other technology, such as DVD players and the Internet, continues to gain in popularity, VCRs may become a thing of the past. However, the information that candidates put on their videos can easily be transferred to other media. Gore's use of his video on his campaign's Internet site is but one example of what is to come in the future.

Chapter Three

How the 2000 Presidential Primary Candidates Were Framed in Their Campaign Videocassettes

Frame analysis allows for a comprehensive description to get at the deeper level of meaning of how presidential primary campaign video-cassettes package candidates. The analysis presented here borrows most from Robert Entman's framing methodology. He argued in "Framing: Toward Clarification of a Fractured Paradigm" (1993) that framing involves "selection and salience" and that frames were "manifested by the presence or absence of certain keywords, stock phrases, stereotyped images, sources of information, and sentences that provide thematically reinforcing clusters of facts or judgments" (p. 52). Entman used this criterion in "Framing U.S. Coverage of International News: Contrasts in Narratives of the KAL and Iran Air Incidents" (1991). He saw the frames that the media created as independent variables that could influence public opinion.

Entman (1993) argued that frames have at least four locations in the communication process. The first location is the communicator, who consciously or unconsciously constructs frames. The second location, the text, contains frames, which include keywords and stereotyped images. Receivers, the third location, then process these frames and mix them with their own personal frames, which are part of the "commonly invoked frames" of the larger culture, which is the fourth location (p. 52).

Analysis of presidential primary videocassettes was also shaped based on Gitlin's frame analysis in *The Whole World Is Watching: Mass Media in the Making and Unmaking of the New Left* (1980). Gitlin focused on understanding the frames constructed by newspapers, magazines, and TV networks in their coverage during the 1960s of the Students for a Democratic Society

(SDS), a left-of-center interest group. Gitlin poured through the archives of media outlets ranging from *The New York Times* to CBS and found they used "framing devices" such as "trivialization," "polarization," and "marginalization" frames to create a story line for how SDS was portrayed to media readers and viewers.

To conduct the frame analysis for this study, two researchers, both trained in qualitative methods and frame analysis, individually viewed all six of the presidential primary campaign videos that were produced during the 2000 presidential election cycle. As a check against the risk of subjective findings, the two researchers came from different backgrounds, with one having more professional and academic experience in political communication than the other.

The guiding research question for the study was: "What were the various frames utilized in the videos of the presidential primary candidates of the 2000 race?" The researchers watched each video several times, using Entman's (1993) framing definition as the basis for analysis. Each video was viewed closely to look for the following:

Keywords, stock phrases, stereotyped images, sources of information, and sentences that provide thematically reinforcing clusters of facts or judgments.

Close attention also was paid to how the videos chose to promote a particular problem definition, causal interpretation, moral evaluation, and/or treatment recommendation for the item described.

In addition, transcripts were made from the videos to aid in the exploration of themes. Notes were taken by the researchers, who cited the keywords, images, moral evaluations, and such that were found in the videos. The notes then were compared. The themes, or frames, that emerge from viewing the videos and transcripts were agreed upon by both researchers.

One of the main purposes of this chapter is to demonstrate the ability of framing to efficiently package complex biographical and issue information about a candidate. Each video was found to contain a predominant frame or frames. Before discussing each candidate's video at length, the predominant framing for each is as follows:

Democrats: Bradley (leadership and electability), Gore (values).

Republicans: Bauer (reclaim Reagan's legacy), Bush (change), Forbes (values and individual freedom), McCain (values).

In addition, one other frame reached across party lines and was found in all six videos: mass media as supplier of validation, or, "I am qualified to be president because the media say I am."

Lastly, the general election campaign films of Gore and Bush were viewed using frame analysis. This analysis is useful in determining what similarities exist between campaign films and primary campaign video-cassettes. The frames are as follows: Gore (values); Bush (values).

BILL BRADLEY'S PRIMARY VIDEO: HE IS A LEADER WHO IS ELECTABLE

Leadership

Bradley's five-minute video, "People Are Talking," highlights his leadership qualities with several clips from CNN's coverage of his presidential an-nouncement speech in Crystal City, Missouri. In the speech he says, "There are two kinds of politicians." He pauses as the crowd laughs. He smiles and con-tinues. "Maybe more," he says. "Those who talk and promise, and those who listen and do. I know which one I am." Bradley's assertion that some politi-cians are just full of talk is meant to draw a contrast to Al Gore, while at the same time show Bradley as a leader. According to Bradley's rhetoric, a leader doesn't merely talk at people, he listens to people and then acts decisively.

"People Are Talking," which is by far the shortest "meet the candidate" video shown during the 2000 presidential primary, has no coherent voice of its own. The video instead strings together clips from several TV news broadcasts that include segments featuring Bradley, his supporters, or commentator analysis of his chances against Vice President Gore.

Leadership on the issues is demonstrated with a clip from PBS's *The Newshour. Wall Street Journal* political analyst Paul Gigot says in an inter-view how Bradley is prepared to act in ways that are unpopular because he feels it it a principled stand that a leader must take. The issues Gigot mentions include child poverty and health care.

In another clip from a news broadcast, Minnesota senator Paul Well-stone, a Bradley supporter, points out that Bradley is a leader who can en-ergize voters who are disaffected by the current leadership and by big-money politics. In a veiled reference to past fund-raising scandals and the need for campaign finance reform, Wellstone notes that a Bradley pres-idency would get the corrosive power of money out of politics, which would allow ordinary citizens to come back into the political arena.

The primary video ends with Bradley's closing remarks at his presiden-tial announcement speech. Bradley says he wants to ensure that everyone has access to the American dream. At one point, Bradley says, "Come with me." He then reaches his arms out toward the crowd, symbolically asking them to follow his leadership. The crowd responds by standing as he ends his remarks.

Electability

Spliced in between footage of Bradley's announcement speech, the primary video provides a number of clips from TV newscasts that address Bradley's ability to get the Democratic nomination and win the White House. For example, the video shows footage from CNN's *Inside Politics*. Anchor Judy Woodruff makes comments that indicate that Bradley's campaign is gaining strength against Gore. She then asks Bill Schneider, a CNN political analyst, if he agrees. He does and adds that Bradley's campaign is also strong in the early, key states. To prove this to the viewers, Schneider discusses the results of a poll of New Hampshire Democrats that demonstrates Bradley's electability. He says Gore's lead over Bradley has been cut from 45 points to just 5 points. Just as dramatic is another poll, this time among New York Democrats, who once supported Gore by an 18-point magin. Schneider then adds that Gore's lead had since evaporated to a mere 2 points.

Next, a voice-over of John McLaughlin, from his TV show *The McLaughlin Group,* is heard while footage is shown of Bradley surrounded by a large crowd of supporters. McLaughlin's voice-over notes that in both New Hampshire and New York, Bradley is nearly tied with Gore. McLaughlin adds that Bradley is now seen by many, including Republicans, as more electable than Gore. Brief footage from Bradley's past, during his New York Knicks days, also is shown. Political commentator Bob Novak is then shown on CNN adding that Democratic sources he has talked to feel that Bradley at the top of the ticket would make it easier for Democrats to take back control of Congress.

Later in the primary video, Schneider is shown on CNN discussing another favorable poll result for Bradley: a September 7–13, 1999, poll for how New York would vote in a match-up between George W. Bush and either Gore or Bradley. Schneider says the polls show Bradley, not Gore, to be the greatest threat to Bush in a general election. "Bradley causes voters who are driven to Bush by Gore to reconsider. So it's official, Bradley can now challenge Gore on electability," Schneider says.

Sometimes the leadership and electablity frames can interact with each other in a way that can seem contradictory. At the beginning of the video, Bradley is shown speaking to a large audience. "I'm more interested in leadership than polls and politics," he says. The crowd cheers. The very next segment in the video is a clip of CNN's *Inside Politics* with Schneider, who notes how poll numbers nationally are favorable for Bradley and that in the key battleground states of New Hampshire and New York, Bradley is almost tied with Gore. So while disregarding polls is a sign of Bradley's leadership, the polls are still vital to establishing his electability.

While little of Bradley's personal biography is outlined in his campaign's primary video, his Democratic opponent, Vice President Gore, uses his video to focus almost solely on his hometown roots.

AL GORE'S PRIMARY VIDEO: HE HAS VALUES

Small-Town Values

Gore's 10-minute primary video, "The Al Gore Story," begins with the camera moving through the green, rolling countryside of Tennessee. Gore's second-grade teacher from Carthage Elementary, an African-American woman named Eleanor Smotherman, sits on her porch and talks about the values of a small town: "I think one of the great things was, the neighborliness of people. Any time there was any need, there were neighbors who would help, both physically and financially."

Dr. Gordon Petty, the Gores' family doctor, then talks about the Gore he remembers growing up in Tennessee: "I was the family doctor, have been for 50 years. On house calls I would sometimes hear, "Hey, Dr. Petty." And I would look over and there would be Al. Sometimes he would go with me on house calls. His father happened to be employed in Washington." Petty's remark that Gore's father "happened to be employed in Washington"—as opposed to saying that he was as a U.S. senator—frames Gore's upbringing as less than privileged.

Gore's primary video uses the small-town values frame to counter perceptions that Gore, who as a child went to private school in Washington, D.C., was more urban than rural. Pauline Gore, his mother, is interviewed in the video and says: "His life was very well balanced in that he had both places to grow up in."

Black and white pictures are shown of a young Al Gore in Tennessee and on Capitol Hill. Old family friends, both male and female, talk about how Gore balanced life in Washington, where his father was a senator, and life back in Tennessee. Jerry Futrell, a family friend, says, "His father wanted to make sure he had a knowledge of the dirt, of the grass roots of what life was all about." Like most of the people interviewed in Gore's video, Futrell is shown outdoors, with trees in the background, to add to the small-town feel of the video. Steve Armistead, another family friend interviewed outdoors, says, "He got his values right here. He got his values out of the hills of Tennessee."

A key small-town values moment is seen in the framing of Gore's military service during the Vietnam War. With several pictures of Gore in military uniform shown during an interview with Jerry Futrell, he says:

The world knew that his father was an opponent of the Vietnam War. But he realized that if he didn't go, somebody else from Smith County [which includes Carthage, Tennessee] would have to take his place. And he stepped up to the plate and said, "I will do what's expected of me."

Gore's political rise from the U.S. House to the Senate to the vice presidency also is framed from the small-town values perspective. Futrell notes: "Of course, after his election to the Congress in 1976, the first thing he did was to hold town hall meetings. He'd go to the grocery store. He'd go to the post office." Hattie Bryant, a retired schoolteacher and African-American woman, adds: "People would come in to meet him and tell their problems, and he would listen to them and talk to them about Social Security and all the things that were involved in their lives." Family friend Hugh Claiborne says, "He would come in and he would introduce himself to every person there and shake their hand."

To visually back up this claim, Gore is then shown shaking hands with elderly residents in town. One elderly man says to him: "I want to tell you that I'm going to vote for you." Gore laughs and says, "OK." The man continues: "'Cause you're doing more for me than I'm doing for you." Gore laughs and says, "I'm working on it."

Complex issue information also is distilled in the form of small-town values. Jean Nelson, president and executive director of The Land Trust for Tennessee, notes that Gore "found ways to listen to what the community needed" on issues such as arms control, technology, and toxic waste. One of the pictures shown during Nelson's remarks is of Gore standing next to a father who is helping his own daughter put a steel cylinder into a local recycling bin.

Self-deprecating humor is sported by Gore to show that, even as vice president, he has not lost his small-town roots. On a clip from *The Late Show with David Letterman*, Gore is asked by Letterman, "What should I call you? Do I call you 'Mr. Vice President?' Do I call you 'Al'?" Gore replies: "'Your Adequacy' is fine." The crowd laughs.

Gore's humor also is displayed through the letter of an eight-year-old boy who wrote to the vice president. Gore is shown reading part of the letter: "I get letters from youngsters and I got one from an eight-year-old boy from Minnesota. He says, 'You are the finest vice president of my time.' It went straight to my head." A small group that is gathered around Gore laughs as he reads the letter.

The primary message, that Gore has not lost his small-town roots, is exemplified in a quote from Dr. Petty, who talks about a conversation he had with Gore the day he was elected vice president of the United States:

At the time they had the countdown party at Little Rock, Al hugged me and said, "We made it." And I said, "Yeah, we made it, but this presents a problem." He said, "What's that?" I said, "It's going to be awful hard to call you Mr. Vice President." And he said, "Let's just keep it the way it always has been."

The primary video ends with a final small-town values comment from Futrell, who notes that Gore likes to refer to the values of Smith County in his speeches. Then the viewer hears a voice-over of Gore, who says, "Smith County is a place where they do know about it when you're born and care about it when you die." Futrell then says, "And to me, everything between that says Al Gore."

President Clinton is shown only briefly in the primary video. In an attempt to keep up the small-town values frame, and distance himself from Washington, D.C., and the scandals of the Clinton administration, Clinton appears in only one scene. Clinton, who is interviewed in the Oval Office, says: "There were two things I wanted most in a vice president. I thought that he would be a very good president. The second reason I picked him was that he knew a lot about things I didn't know much about, and that together we would measurably increase the impact of the White House in a positive way."

A Father and Husband

Gore's video includes values-validating interviews with his wife Tipper and daughter Karenna. Tipper Gore, who is interviewed outdoors in a blue button-down shirt, says: "When I first met him I was 16. I met him at a party, and I remember looking at him and I thought, 'Wow, he's really good looking.'" Black and white and color photos of their courtship are shown during her remarks.

In the primary video, Tipper Gore shares intimate personal emotions about her husband in an attempt to play up the values frame: "My favorite picture of him is one that I took of him several years ago when I was a student of photography. And one of the assignments was to take a picture of someone and let the picture show that they love you. The picture is of Al shaving and turning and looking at me. And that's my favorite. You can just see the love in his eyes." The photo Tipper Gore refers to is shown during her remarks.

Jerry Futrell validates Gore's credentials as a good father: "Ever since Karenna came along he's been a dedicated and devoted father. And as the others came along, Kristen and Sarah and Albert, he developed a real feel for his family."

Karenna Gore, his eldest daughter, gives a personal account of what Gore was like as father: "He was working hard when I was very little. He worked as a reporter at night and was taking classes during the day. And we were very excited when he came home. He had great games he would play with us. He was very creative. He would tell us stories and lay [sic] down with us. . . . My dad has a really great sense of humor. Sometimes very unique and unexpected." Karenna Gore also talks about the closeness she shares with her father today. She says, "My wedding day is a really special memory. It was a very fun time, but at the same time it was very emotional. My father gave me great guidance, and I knew he would always be there for me." Photos of Gore and his daughter talking are shown during her remarks.

The primary video also finds ways to convert the husband/father values frame into political currency. Karenna links her father's private and public life when she says, "What motivates my father in what he does is making changes that make people's everyday lives better. And he takes the values that he's taught us and are important to him and tries to put them to work for everyone." Tipper Gore adds: "The person I know is a kind, compassionate person. He has a powerful mind, he's a great leader, but the most important thing is that he's a great father and good husband."

Gore also uses self-deprecating humor in the father/husband values frame. In one scene, Gore is shown talking with supporters. He says: "Tipper and I are expecting our first grandchild at the end of June. And I've been getting some granddad advice, and I'm just glad to find out that you don't have to look old to be a granddad." The crowd laughs.

The video "The Al Gore Story" tells a mostly personal tale and avoids detailed issue discussions. On the Republican side, the campaign of conservative activist Gary Bauer provides an example of how primary videocassettes can be used to outline a variety of issue appeals.

GARY BAUER'S PRIMARY VIDEO: HE WILL RECLAIM RONALD REAGAN'S LEGACY

Bauer's 19-minute video, "Who I Am and What I Believe," tries visually and verbally to cast the former Reagan administration official as the heir apparent to the legacy of President Ronald Reagan. To reinforce this point, Bauer's video even borrows some footage and music from Reagan's 1984 general election campaign film, "A New Beginning."

The video begins with footage of the Reagan years: Reagan taking the presidential oath of office, Reagan getting aboard Marine One and waving. In a voice-over, Bauer says, "He was the most successful Republican candidate in decades and one of our greatest presidents. Yet 10 years after he waved goodbye and boarded Marine One for the last time, I fear that our party has forgotten the important lessons that he taught us." The video then cuts to Bauer standing next to a screen that shows images of Reagan campaigning, an elderly man raising and saluting an American flag, a mother with her child, then kids pledging allegiance to a flag in school. He says, "In the 1980s, Ronald Reagan built a great majority by reaching out to all Americans, not just to Republicans, but to Democrats and Independents who shared his vision for America: smaller government, lower taxes, a strong national defense, and policies that put people and families first."

Bauer then argues that Reagan's legacy and America's future are in jeopardy, saying, "Some in our party even say we must abandon our stand on traditional values and turn our back on the very issues and people that won Ronald Reagan two landslide victories." The video then cuts to Bauer directly addressing the camera:

I'm Gary Bauer and I say they're wrong. Now more than ever we need to embrace principles that will bring us together, not drive us apart. A message that will unite social and fiscal conservatives. A platform that is not only politically effective, but economically sound and morally responsible. And we can do all this without compromising our principles. That's why I'm running for president of the United States. I don't go into this campaign with any misconceptions. I know it will be difficult. Standing up for what's right often is. But I simply refuse to believe that we have to abandon our principles in order to win elections. It's time to lead the Republican Party back to the core principles that made us proud and strong. It's time to reclaim the legacy of Ronald Reagan.

Bauer's personal and public biography also is framed within the context of Reagan's legacy. After a male narrator recounts Bauer's upbringing in Newport, Kentucky, Bauer adds that watching Reagan's 1964 nationally televised speech, "A Time for Choosing" was a turning point in his life. Black and white footage of the speech is shown during Bauer's remarks.

The primary video then lists Bauer's government service credentials, which revolve around the Reagan administration. As he talks about working in the Office of Policy Development, and as undersecretary of education at the Department of Education, many photos are shown of Bauer with Reagan at Cabinet meetings and in the Oval Office. Bauer then tries to show how he was an integral part of Reagan's legacy: "When I worked for Ronald Reagan, on my recommendation, he instituted an executive order that required the bureaucracy in Washington to ask what the impact would be on the American family of any new proposal, any new bureaucratic ideas that comes out of this city." The narrator notes that after the Reagan administration, Bauer joined the Family Research Council, a lobbying organization, and wrote several books on children and family issues. He also formed the Campaign for Working Families, which became the sixth largest political action committee in the nation.

The issues segment of Bauer's primary video is rich in allusions to Reagan's legacy. During this portion of the video, Bauer, who often is shown being interviewed in an official-looking office, notes how Reagan used issues to unify the GOP's base and reach out to what would later be called "Reagan Democrats." He says:

You know, up until Ronald Reagan, my party, the Republican Party, had a fine economic message in many ways. It was tough on foreign policy issues, but it wasn't winning elections. And the reason it wasn't winning elections was that it didn't have this other part of the program, that is these issues that revolve around family, that revolve around what we want to be teaching our children, what kind of culture we're going to have. Ronald Reagan brought those things. He talked about them without shame or embarrassment and because he did that, millions of people switched out of the Democratic Party. Midwestern Catholic, Southern Evangelicals came to the party for the first time in decades and made us in many ways the governing party in the United States during those years. I think the Republican Party needs to stand for a set of ideas: lower taxes, smaller government, family values, respect for life, and a strong American foreign policy built on American values. Those are the things I'm going to argue for. I believe if my party embraces those things it will, in fact, be the governing party of the United States well into the next century.

Bauer frames many complex issues as a choice between abandoning or returning to the values of President Reagan. In one segment, he talks about conventional military issues and also about the need to build a defense shield against nuclear missiles:

Reagan discovered that we did not have a ballistic missile defense system. It was when he was still governor. He went out to visit our defense command center in Colorado, and he asked what would be done if a missile, an enemy missile, was headed toward the United States. And he was told, "Well, we would call the mayor of that city and tell him he's got 15 minutes to evacuate." Unfortunately, here we are many years later, and we still cannot knock down an ICBM headed toward an American city. The Clinton administration began, as many of us still remember, with the great debate of whether there should be open homosexuality in the military. And then he took the Reagan Navy, which was up to about 600 or 700 ships, and he's taken it right back down to the 300s again.

The divisive issue of abortion also is framed as a choice between abandoning or reclaiming Reagan's legacy. On this issue, Bauer's comments are directed more toward Republican Party faithful than political independents. Bauer argues that Reagan's pro-life stand on abortion was not only morally correct, but politically appropriate: "Reagan as president wrote a little book on the sanctity of human life, and why in his view that issue about how we treat defenseless unborn children would define America and what the founding fathers meant when they talked about life and liberty. That was the Reagan that I admired. That was the Reagan I wanted to work for. And that was the Reagan the American people gave two landslide elections to. My party would do well to get back to those values."

At the end of the primary video, Bauer speaks directly to the camera, asking viewers to help him personally and financially. He contrasts the legacy of President Clinton to that of President Reagan, and he asks his viewers to help him reclaim the legacy of Reagan: "Today our nation is at a crossroads. Will we continue down our current path following the example set by Bill Clinton? Or will we, the great conservative majority, stand up once and for all and make our country the shining city on a hill that Ronald Reagan always dreamed it would be."

Bauer's video, which is stridently conservative in tone, stands in stark contrast to the video of Texas governor George W. Bush. His video shows the softer side of the candidate and the GOP.

GEORGE W. BUSH'S PRIMARY VIDEO: HE IS A CHANGE

Change for the Republican Party

In George W. Bush's 13-minute primary video, "A Fresh Start," the Texas governor is framed as someone who will expand the base of the

GOP and go out of his way to reach out—literally and metaphorically—to all types of voters. Bush often is shown shaking hands with—and even hugging—large crowds of supporters, many of whom are African American and Hispanic. In one scene, a Hispanic woman runs up to Bush and hugs him as he is walking in a parade. Then a Hispanic woman is shown bear-hugging Bush, who is sitting on a park bench; Bush faces the camera and grins. In another scene, he kisses a young Hispanic girl who is dressed in a traditional Mexican costume.

Laura Bush joins her husband in many of the scenes where he is reaching out to minorities. In one shot, Bush and his wife are sitting on the steps of a school, talking and laughing with an ethnically diverse group of children. The next shot is of the whole group of them—George W. and Laura included—waving at the camera. In addition, there are many other scenes where large groups of minority children are shown playing and laughing in front of the camera. This acknowledgment of the camera strips away any of the subtlety of Bush's message that he's a candidate who's reaching out to minorities.

Most of the visual imagery in the first part of the video comes from re-cycled footage of Bush's 1994 and 1998 Texas governor races. In one scene, a crowd of teenage supporters is shown, with the camera focusing on one African-American teenager holding a "Bush for governor" sign high above his head. Using footage from his past Texas campaigns also makes it easier to display Bush's minority outreach activities. The primary video's more current footage of Bush's 2000 presidential campaigning in New Hampshire and Iowa shows the candidate in a more ethnically ho-mogenous setting.

The primary video, which uses no narrator, stays mostly silent for the first seven minutes. Instead, viewers are treated to a barrage of images—accompanied by music—of Bush in minority outreach mode. These many images are strung together quickly, one after another. Throughout much of the video, the camera moves in a jerky motion similar to the camera movement seen on the TV show *NYPD Blue*. This effect gives viewers the sense of a campaign in constant motion and also allows the video to in-corporate as many images of Bush in different settings as possible.

Then, in the middle of the video, the Bush campaign tries to translate these multiple images of minority outreach into political currency. The video notes how Bush's success in reaching out to nontraditional Republi-cans has helped change the Texas Republican Party. This message, in turn, suggests how Bush can change the national Republican Party, making it larger, more inclusive, and more powerful. Superimposed over footage of Bush and Laura at a campaign rally, are these words:

On November 3, 1998 George W. Bush was reelected Governor of Texas with 69% of the vote. It was the first time in history a Texas Governor was elected to consec-utive 4-year terms. Bush was reelected with the support of Hispanics (49%), African Americas (27%), Democrats (31%), Women (66%), Independents (73%).

Governor Bush helped carry 17 statewide Republicans into office, and today for the first time in Texas history, all 27 statewide elected officials are Republicans.

The primary video also chronicles Bush's first days campaigning for president in Iowa and New Hampshire through the frame of "Bush, the man to expand the base of the GOP." After Bush and his wife are shown getting off a plane together and waving to supporters, footage is shown of Bush kissing an elderly lady on the cheek at a rally and talking with African-American schoolchildren. There's also a shot of a Catholic priest at a rally wearing a Bush sticker and holding an American flag. Reaching out to Catholic voters illustrates Bush's attempt to appeal to all types of voters, from racial minorities to a religious minority that holds much political sway in several key midwestern battleground states.

In the same way that Gore uses humor to bolster his "values" frame, Bush uses humor to reinforce his image as someone who reaches out to minorities. In one humorous moment, after showing a picture book to children in a classroom, Bush is shown joking around with an African-American boy. While the boy is not looking, Bush taps him on the shoulder. Bush then looks away as if he did not tap the boy on the shoulder. The boy looks around to see who tapped him. He then looks at Bush. They laugh.

One scene in the video exemplifies Bush's hunger to reach out and touch voters, almost in a Clintonesque way. Bush, who is shaking hands at a rally, sees a man in the crowd who has his back turned to him. Bush leans over, taps him on the shoulder to get his attention, smiles, and shakes his hand.

Media validation also reinforces the frame that Bush is a change for the GOP. News clips are shown from many publications, including "I've been covering candidates campaigning here since 1980, and I've never seen anything like this," from David Kotok of *The Omaha World News.* Another news clip, from *The Washington Post,* says, "Everywhere he went, Bush was greeted by large crowds—much larger than normal for so early in the campaign—and the audience seemed eager to like him."

Change for the Country

The Bush video starts with him sitting comfortably on a couch in a Western style, blue, open-collar shirt, talking about why he believes he can make "a positive difference" in politics. Bush says later in the video that his campaign offers "a fresh start after a season of cynicism."

The last third of the video is a variation of a "talking head ad," with Bush giving a speech to a Midwest crowd in a field with a red tractor behind him. In this setting, he talks about issues such as education, the economy, and character. He starts by making the point that the country needs to rethink its definition of prosperity: "I'm running because I want America to be prosperous. But I want there to be a purpose to prosperity. Prosperity alone is simple materialism. The worth of America has never been proven with cities of gold, but by citizens of character. Prosperity with a purpose is to make sure that no one is left behind. That no one feels left out. And I'm running because I want our political party to match a conservative mind with a compassionate heart."

Bush argues that the nation's current cynicism can be changed through responsibility and "citizens of character." He also says that government has a role to play in bringing about these changes:

My dream is to usher in what I call "the responsibility era," an era that will stand in stark contrast to the last few decades, which has clearly said, "If it feels good, do it, and if you got a problem, blame somebody else." Government can help usher in the responsibility era. We can pass laws that clearly say to citizens, "You are responsible for the decisions you make in life." The federal government can help states change their juvenile justice codes so we can say to our children, "We love you a lot, but discipline and love go hand-in-hand. We care for you, but you got to understand with certainty that there will be bad consequences for bad behavior."

Bush also promises that the tone of his campaign, and the manner in which he runs for office, will represent a real change for America: "I'm going to run a campaign that is positive and hopeful and optimistic, and I want to run a campaign that lifts the spirit of America and reinvigorates our soul. I'm going to prove that you can win a campaign by being a compassionate conservative without sacrificing principle. And we will show that after a time of tarnished ideals, politics can be higher and better." The video then shows a news clip from the *The Boston Globe* to validate Bush's "compassionate conservative claim": "Bush will add a sense of civility badly needed in a national campaign ... he is a welcome sight for an electorate that has grown too accustomed to negative news."

Unlike the primary campaign videos of Gore, Bauer, Forbes, and McCain, Bush's video never addresses the candidate's personal or family history prior to entering public service. Bush's children, and his famous father and mother, are seen in brief shots but have no speaking roles.

STEVE FORBES'S PRIMARY VIDEO: HE HAS FAMILY VALUES AND WILL EXPAND INDIVIDUAL FREEDOM

The biographical and issues segments of Steve Forbes's 18-minute video, "A Rebirth of Freedom," mostly use separate frames. While Forbes's personal history, as well as the history of his famous family, are presented through the "values" frame, Forbes's political issues segment is presented in great detail through the frame of "the rights of the individual" and "individual freedom."

Family Values

The biographical segment of Forbes's video shows Forbes speaking at the pulpit of a church mostly populated by African Americans. He tries to connect with the audience by talking about his family's humble beginnings. He says, "I've lived the American Dream, and I've lived it because of my grandfather. My grandfather came to this country 90 years ago. He was an immigrant from Scotland." Visuals shown during part of his remarks include an old black and white Forbes family photo from the turn of the century. Also, bagpipe music is played during this segment to reinforce the visual and verbal message of the family's Scottish immigrant roots. Many members of the Forbes clan, including Steve Forbes's brothers Bob, Tim, and Kip, appear in the video to validate Forbes—and reinforce the family values frame.

Steve Forbes then explains how their grandfather, B.C. Forbes, created *Forbes* magazine in 1917, the same year as the Russian Revolution. An early *Forbes* magazine cover shows the subhead "Devoted to Doers and Doings." Forbes then smiles and says, "Wherever my grandfather is today, he must be delighted that his creation outlasted Lenin's creation."

Steve Forbes's brothers then note how through the value of hard work, Steve earned his way at *Forbes* magazine—from working in the mail room at 16 to eventually running the company and making it more successful than it was under his famous father. A number of visual images, including old photos of Steve Forbes working as a reporter, reinforce the idea that Forbes worked his way to the top.

Bob Forbes talks about the family experiences he and his brothers had growing up and links them to the values frame. During remarks where he notes how the family loved to take vacations together, old family vacation photos are shown; one photo is of the Forbes brothers in matching cowboy hats. Steve Forbes's values as a father and husband are validated by testimonial quotes from daughters Moira and Sabina.

Expand Individual Freedom

Validation of Forbes on political issues relating to freedom comes from many sources, including Caspar Weinberger, secretary of defense under President Reagan, economist Walter Williams, and former British prime minister Margaret Thatcher. In one scene, Forbes and Thatcher are walking together and talking to one another at a large event, which is decorated with American and British flags. Thatcher is then shown speaking at that event: "So I would say that Reagan conservatives, Thatcher conservatives and Steve Forbes conservatives all believe in the same fundamental things: the right to life, and to liberty and to freedom."

The video addresses Forbes's main issue stands—such as reforming health care, Social Security, public schools, and the tax code—from the perspective of freedom and personal choice. On the issue of privatizing Social Security, Forbes frames his controversial proposal as a way to expand the personal financial freedom of people, especially the young: "All we have to do is go back to a very basic American principle: It's called freedom. And with freedom, responsibility. What about young people? Shouldn't they have freedom to have their own retirement accounts away from the Washington politicians on Social Security?" Footage shown during part of his remarks—a young married couple at home with their three kids—reinforces the point that young people need the flexibility and freedom to care for themselves and their loved ones. Also, man-on-the-street type interviews are used to validate Forbes's policy agenda. One unidentified young woman says, "For me to be paying out of my paycheck to the Social Security system, not knowing that anything will be there for myself when I retire, is unsettling." Then the video cuts to Forbes explaining his policies from the pulpit of an African-American church. The church crowd claps as Forbes makes his case.

Forbes next takes on the issue of medical savings accounts (MSAs), which he argues should be created nationwide to help deal with rising health care costs. He says, "Why shouldn't we have a simple principle: patient in charge of health care?" The video then cuts to an interview with an unidentified baby boomer-age woman outside: "If you put back into the hands of individuals their purchasing of health care, you will see a big difference." Here again, the framing is clear. The complex issue of medical savings accounts is packaged as a simple decision to "put back into the hands of individuals" their freedom with regard to health care choices.

The video frames Forbes's call for a flat tax, perhaps the issue most closely associated with the candidate, as an issue of personal freedom from the federal government power structure. An interview with George Mason University economist Walter Williams validates Forbes's claim: "A simpler tax code where you tell a person, 'Look, take your gross income, multiply it by .17, .16, whatever the particular number, and send it in.' I mean you're talking about a half-hour's worth of work as opposed to several days, hiring an accountant, hiring lawyers."

The issue of school vouchers also is framed as a choice between personal freedom and interference from outsiders. Forbes argues he will give parents "the freedom to choose schools that work for their kids." He contrasts his vision with the current public school system where such choices are left up to "a self-anointed and appointed bureaucracy."

While Forbes's video details the candidate's biography and issue stands, there is a slight disconnect between the frames used in each of these sections. Arizona senator John McCain's video takes a different approach by connecting the candidate's personal history to his political positions.

JOHN McCAIN'S PRIMARY VIDEO: HE HAS VALUES

Both McCain's biographical and issues information are told through the values frame. McCain is presented as a man who will do what is "right" for his family and his country no matter who or what gets in his way, whether it be friend or foe.

Moral Character

McCain's 11-minute video, "The Character to Do What's Right, the Courage to Fight for It," opens with an unidentified male narrator: "At a time when America is searching for heroes to lead us, it has the genuine article in John McCain. Whether as a navy pilot in Vietnam or in the U.S. Senate, his whole life, he's thrived on challenges. And he's always put America's interest ahead of his own. Now, John McCain looks ahead to his greatest challenge yet as he runs for president. To restore integrity to the office, reform government, and renew the American dream."

Much visual imagery is shown during the narrator's remarks to reinforce McCain's heroic values frame. For the most part, this imagery connects McCain to his service in Vietnam, with old film footage and several old photos of McCain in his pilot's uniform. Then McCain is seen saluting, walking down an airplane as he returns from Vietnam. To bring McCain's image into the present, the Arizona senator also is shown shaking hands with voters in a town square setting, with the American flag flapping in the background.

The first half of the video provides McCain's personal history, which the narrator recounts through the values frame: "A son of the Navy, John Sidney McCain was born into a family where duty, honor, and country were articles of faith." McCain's decision to fight in Vietnam is framed as a family values moment: "Nearly all the men in the McCain family had made their reputations during wartime. And John wanted to keep faith with them. A veteran aircraft carrier pilot, he asked to go to Vietnam." The family values frame is bolstered visually with old family photos of several generations of McCain men, mostly in uniform.

The narrator continues the values frame as he recounts how McCain almost lost his life during an accident aboard the U.S.S. *Forrestal* in July 1967. Visual imagery includes archival back and white footage of McCain during the disaster, which started when a missile accidentally fired from a nearby plane and struck a fuel tank. The narrator notes that as McCain tried to "help a fellow pilot" he was "blown back 10 feet when more bombs exploded. It took 24 hours to contain the inferno on the *Forrestal*. But not before 134 men lost their lives and more than 120 planes were destroyed." The denouement to this story further strengthens McCain's values image: "After the *U.S.S. Forrestal* disaster, McCain could have returned home, but instead, he volunteered for more combat duty."

McCain is framed as the hero who will do what is right for his country even when he has the opportunity to just do what is right for himself. This information becomes all the more poignant in the next segment of McCain's video, which tells the tale of his five and a half years in a Vietnamese prisoner of war camp called the "Hanoi Hilton":

In the early morning of October 26, 1967, Lt. Commander McCain departed for his twenty-third bombing mission over North Vietnam. He and his fellow pilots were targeting a power plant in the center of Hanoi. As McCain was completing his bombing mission, a Soviet-made surface-to-air missile struck his plane, sheering off the right wing. McCain ejected as his plane spiraled violently to earth. The force of the ejection knocked him unconscious. Both of his arms and one leg were broken. He came to as he plunged into a lake near his bombing target. Quickly, an angry mob gathered seeking retribution for the reign of bombs. They broke his shoulder with a rifle butt and bayoneted him repeatedly. McCain was loaded onto a truck and delivered to the infamous and hated Hanoi Hilton. McCain's condition deteriorated badly. His fellow POWs, shocked at his appearance, thought McCain was near death. But they were determined he survive.

The visuals used during the narrator's remarks—footage of a pilot being shot at and ejecting from a plane—got the McCain campaign in trouble. The scenes are from stock Pentagon footage, not from McCain's own incident, as the viewer is led to believe (Kranish, 1999).

McCain's video expands on the value of selflessness as the narrator notes how McCain refused early release, which was offered because McCain's father was a high ranking Navy official, and chose instead to be treated like his fellow POWs. In a present-day interview, McCain talks about how the value of "faith" helped him overcome the hardships of being a prisoner of war: "There are three keys to successful survival in a prison camp situation such as I and my friends were in. First is faith in God, the other is faith in your fellow prisoners—you have to have faith that your fellow prisoners were working just as hard as you were to resist—and faith in one's country.

As photos of McCain's homecoming are shown, the narrator notes that McCain had to undergo "extensive physical rehabilitation," due to the wounds he suffered as a POW. It is also revealed that McCain divorced his wife after returning home: "Sadly, like a lot of prisoners of war, John's marriage ended several years later."

McCain's love story relationship with his second wife, Cindy, is then told through the frame of a husband and father with strong values. The narrator notes how because Cindy McCain wanted to raise their young children in Arizona, John McCain "maintained a ritual" of flying home every weekend to be there for them. A home movie showing McCain bouncing one of his young children on his knee reinforces the family friendly image. Says Cindy McCain: "John is a loving, kind, strong father. He's involved in every way with these children, even with our odd circumstance of not living on the same coast at all times. He understands the importance of being there and being relied upon and also has taken an active and equal role in all the things that aren't so fun, like discipline and homework, and all the things that take place in a daily life of a busy family."

Her values-laden description of McCain is further reinforced as she explains how, as part of a medical team in Bangladesh, she brought back to the United States an injured child, Bridget, whom they later adopted. She says: "I showed up in Phoenix and John whispered, 'Where is she going to go?' And I said, 'Well, I thought maybe she'd go to our house.' And he said, 'Well, I had a feeling that might be the case. She's welcome in our home.'"

Political Courage

The second half of the video is devoted to spelling out in detail McCain's stands on various issues. His policy positions—ranging from federal government cost containment to Internet filtering technology to campaign finance reform—are framed as battles McCain is selflessly waging on behalf of the country. As the narrator puts it: "On issue after issue, John McCain defies the special interests even when it hurts him politically." McCain's efforts in the U.S. Senate to limit so-called pork-barrel legislation is framed as a "one-man crusade." The narrator notes that McCain's nickname is "the sheriff on wasteful spending." This verbal message also is made visually with footage of McCain walking proudly, with the Capitol dome behind him. The camera angle is looking up at him, making McCain appear larger than life. The words: "The sheriff on wasteful spending" is then superimposed on the screen. The narrator notes that this is one of many offensives in McCain's crusade for America:

McCain knows that cutting government waste means we can lower the tax burden on America's families and eliminate the inheritance tax and the unfair marriage penalty. Save Social Security once and for all by guaranteeing that all Social Security funds will be spent only on Social Security and kept out of the hands of politicians. But most of all, John McCain worries about what kind of country we're leaving our children. He's protecting them from the evils of Internet smut by promoting the use of filtering technology.

The McCain video goes out of its way to use the values frame to efficiently package the complex issue of campaign finance reform, which is politically unpopular among rank-and-file Republicans. After linking the concept of campaign finance reform to the other government reforms previously mentioned, the narrator notes that McCain "dares Washington to support his efforts to break the stranglehold that special interests and their money have over the political process." Seen from this perspective, the

McCain/Feingold campaign finance legislation is framed as just one more courageous, selfless battle to save America from her enemies.

At the end of the video, McCain directly addresses the camera. He says he needs personal and financial support in order to "make our country live up to its reputation as the land of the free."

ALL PRIMARY VIDEOS: I AM QUALIFIED TO BE PRESIDENT BECAUSE THE MEDIA SAY I AM

Some candidates used the media as a supplier of validation more than others. Bradley's video spends the most time, as a percentage of the video, showing clips from various media sources to validate his claims of leadership and electability. In one scene, journalist Bob Novak is shown on NBC's *Meet the Press* arguing that wherever Bradley campaigns, his poll numbers rise. Host Tim Russert adds that Bradley is an outsider and a viable alternative to Gore.

The video for Gore, who was a reporter at *The (Nashville) Tennessean* before entering politics, provides testimonial interviews with two major figures at *The Tennessean*. Editor Frank Sutherland is interviewed in his office. "When he came, he didn't want anything to do with government and politics. But the more that he wrote stories about people and their relationships, the more he found out about how government affected their lives or didn't affect their lives when it ought to.... I think one of the reasons he decided to go into politics and leave journalism is that he thought he could even have more of an effect on the system if he got involved politically."

Gore's primary video also shows clips from his news stories, as well as photos of Gore as a reporter at his typewriter and taking notes. John Seigenthaler, former editor and publisher of *The Tennessean*, talks about how the skills Gore learned as a reporter have served him well in politics: "He was covering the metro city council in what was one of the most important news stories in our community. And he broke it. And to this day, there is a healthy, wholesome feeling in our community because of what Al was able to do.... The best of Al Gore the reporter frequently shows up in the best of Al Gore the politician. The ability to ask sensitive questions. The ability, at times, to ask the blunt, hard, questions—I mean it's there."

Gore's video may have used too much media validation. Shortly after the video's release, Sutherland had to issue an apology to the Gannett Co., the owner of the newspaper, because of concerns that he violated its ethics policy, which mandates that journalists maintain impartiality in political matters (Taylor, 1999).

On the Republican side, Bush and Bauer make the most use of the media. Bush's primary video uses media validation as much as Gore's, but in a different way. Bush's video shows numerous clips from various media outlets—such as *The New York Times, The Boston Globe, The Washington Post, USA Today, Fortune, Business Week,* and several Texas newspapers—to back up his political claims. Several of the numerous headlines include:

"Since George W. Bush took office in 1995, employment has grown by 15%"—*Fortune Magazine*

"Violent juvenile crimes have decreased 30% and Texas welfare rolls have declined 47%"—*Fortune Magazine*

"Tort reform to give Texas savings on 1998 insurance"—*San Antonio Express-News*

"Bush has a record of cutting taxes, remaking welfare, and toughening the juvenile justice system"—*USA Today*

"...a personable and charismatic campaigner"— *New York Times*

"Bush will add a sense of civility badly needed in a national campaign...he is a welcome sight for an electorate that has grown too accustomed to negative news"—*The Boston Globe*

"On a national level, the success of Bush's education initiatives is crucial to recasting the Republican Party in his 'Compassionate Conservative' image"—*Business Week*

"George W. Bush is the GOP's best hope for 2000"—*Fortune Magazine*

On the issue of education, George W. and Laura Bush are shown speaking to children in a classroom while the words "Education Week awarded Texas an A- for moving the state's minority student test scores to the top of the nation" run across the screen. Then there's a clip from *The Austin American-Statesman*: "Texas schools earn highest marks ever." Later in the video, Bush talks about how "failed schools in this great land create two societies: one that reads and one that can't, one that dreams and one that doesn't. It is the burden on the conscience of a great nation." Bush continues: "It is the real challenge to America's great heart. And the next president must close the gap of hope if we're to have the kind of twenty-first century that all of us want to have for everybody." The video then fades to a clip from *Business Week*: "Is Bush's record on education really that good? In short, yes."

Like Bush, Bauer uses quotes from newspapers and magazines to validate his political claims. In one segment of the video where Bauer argues that America has been led astray and needs to get back to "traditional values," several newspaper clips are shown as proof. The headlines cover many issues, such as: "Baby found in trash," "GOP in mood to compromise," "Russians said to sell missiles to Saddam," "On average, every day a killer is free," "Peace talks adjourn in disarray," "Target America; Need for a missile defense system." Also, there is a *New York Daily News* cover with Clinton on the cover and the headline "Liar, Liar."

Bauer's video differs from Bush's in that Bauer uses footage of himself on C-Span and other media outlets to prove that he is a national figure worthy of national office. He also is shown on CNN's *Crossfire*, PBS's *The Newshour*, CBS's *Face the Nation*, NBC's *Today Show*, CNN's *Larry King Live*, ABC's *This Week with David Brinkley*, CNBC's *Hardball*, CNN's *Both Sides with Jesse Jackson*, and NBC's *Meet the Press*. A male narrator notes: "As a frequent guest on national television news programs, Gary Bauer has demonstrated that he is a committed candidate, in command of the issues, and in touch with the American electorate."

Like Bauer, Steve Forbes is shown on *Meet the Press*, which seems to be the political news show of choice for the candidate videos. Forbes also is shown on the cover of *Time* and *Newsweek* magazines promoting his flat tax plan. On the *Newsweek* cover, Forbes is ripping an IRS tax form. The headline says: "Steve Forbes Wants a Flat Tax. Do You? RRRRip!" Forbes's presidential campaign activities also are given credibility by the media. In one scene, Forbes is interviewed by a TV reporter who is standing next to a grain silo in the Midwest. The reporter notes that Forbes had just spent time with some local farmers. Like Gore, Forbes cites his personal media experience as one of his qualifications to be president. With regard to *Forbes* magazine, family members make the point that it was Steve who was instrumental in keeping the magazine successful after Malcolm Forbes died.

Forbes's video also lists Forbes's tenure as chairman of the board that oversaw Radio Free Europe during the Reagan administration as a key presidential credential. Frank Shakespeare, former ambassador to Portugal and the Vatican, notes that Radio Free Europe's mission was to communicate Western news to people in Communist countries. Shakespeare praises Forbes's ability to "steep himself in the knowledge of these countries, the issues at play." He adds: "By coincidence he did it at maybe the most sensitive time in history." Visuals accompanying Shakespeare's remarks include footage of the Berlin Wall coming down.

Then Forbes talks about what political lessons he learned from this media experience. He notes that while Radio Free Europe's mission was to fight the war of ideas with words and not bullets, the struggle was still real and he was proud to be a part of it. Caspar Weinberger then appears in the video to validate Forbes's claims. Weinberger says the image of the United States was greatly improved due to the broadcasts of Radio Free Europe during Forbes's tenure. Kip Forbes then talks about the larger issues of his brother's media experience.

John McCain's video uses media validation least, though the technique is still effective. Toward the beginning of the video, the narrator says: "His whole life, he's thrived on challenges." The accompanying visual image is McCain on the cover of *National Journal* magazine with the headline "A Maverick Takes on the Senate and Looks to 2000." This visual cue of a "maverick" who "takes on" challenges fits nicely with the overall theme of the video. In the segment devoted to explaining McCain's heroics during the disaster aboard the U.S.S *Forrestal,* newspaper clips of the event are shown to back up the claims made about the accident.

CONCLUSIONS AND IMPLICATIONS FOR THE PRIMARY VIDEOS OF 2000

This study explores the types of frames constructed by one type of political advertising: presidential primary campaign videos. Each video was found to package its candidate in a unique way, though some videos shared common frames, and the use of the media as a supplier of validation for their claims is seen in all of the videos.

The "values" frame, seen in the videos of Gore, McCain, and Forbes, mostly is used to highlight the strong family ties the candidate has. George W. Bush's video, which ignores Bush's personal history prior to becoming governor, fails to provide a similar opportunity to display family values. Bauer's video also could be seen as part of the "values" frame, though the video's visual and verbal adherence to reclaiming Reagan's legacy seems to be the dominant story line.

The primary videos' use of the media as a supplier of validation is also worth noting. Many political leaders like to use the print and broadcast media as something of a punching bag—and at times, something of a scapegoat. This can be especially true during the heat of a presidential race. Yet the message in these direct-mail videos is that viewers should trust what they hear in the media. Also, as is the case in Gore's video, the role of the journalist is compared favorably to the role of the politician: both jobs are a form of noble public service. Bauer seems to gain the most from the use of media validation. By inundating viewers with image after image of Bauer on national TV news shows, the little-known Republican candidate is able to show himself as a nationally known and well-respected commentator.

One of the main purposes of this chapter was to demonstrate the ability of framing to efficiently package complex biographical and issue information about a candidate. Kahneman and Tversky (1984) showed through experiments that the process of framing entails increasing awareness of certain issues and directing attention away from other issues. How the McCain campaign framed his divorce is an instructive example of Kahneman and Tversky's point. By framing the divorce as just one more sad chapter in McCain's character-building prisoner of war experience, one is invited to feel sympathy for McCain and is directed away from thoughts of who was to blame for the breakup.

Political advertising research can be expanded by scholarship on candidate videos. As Devlin (1994) found with the 1992 primary TV ads, candidates who retain a fixed image fare well in comparison with candidates who produce multiple images. Future research should look at image consistency between the candidates' videocassettes and their TV ads. This also raises the issue of frame consistency between media coverage and political ads. For example, George W. Bush, whose primary video frames him as a man who reaches out to nontraditional Republican voters, had his racial and religious tolerance questioned in primary campaign press coverage. Future research should examine voter effects when inconsistency exists between videocassette and media coverage frames.

Campaign videocassette research can advance framing scholarship and has several implications for the study of political advertising. Some political advertising scholars see framing as part of agenda setting (Ghanem, 1997), while others disagree (Kosicki, 1993). Either way, the two theories can be seen as sharing at least one similarity. In the same way that agenda-setting research was first used to describe the impact of journalists and later expanded to include the agenda-setting role of political advertising (Roberts and McCombs, 1994), framing's journalist-centered approach can be enriched by broadening framing research to include the story lines constructed in political ads.

Research in this study also seeks to add to emerging scholarship on framing theory. Scheufele's (1999) four-cell framing typology (p. 108) divides description of individual-based and mass media-based frames into independent and dependent variables. Under the heading of the media as the independent variable, he contends that researchers should ask, "What kinds of media frames influence the audience's perception of certain issues, and how does the process work?" With regard to individual frames as the dependent variable, he asks, "Which factors influence the establishment of individual frames of reference, or are individual frames simply replications of media frames?" Framing research on presidential primary campaign videos contributes to Scheufele's process model of framing (p. 114), which is designed to examine four processes: frame building, frame setting, individual-level effects of framing, and links between individual frames and media frames. With regard to frame building, he argues that the frames journalists construct are more likely to be influenced by political actors and interest groups for "relatively new issues, that is, issues for which no frames have yet been established" (p. 116). As noted earlier, presidential primary campaign videos are mailed out during the early days of the primary campaign, which for many candidates is the first time they receive national press scrutiny. Seen from this perspective, candidate videocassettes may be a significant contributor to the frame-building process of journalists during the primary campaign season.

It needs to be noted that this research is exploratory in nature and is the first step toward analyzing the larger framing process in political advertising. Also, many facets of the presidential primary videos also need to be addressed, including how useful voters find them to be and what role the videos play in each campaign's advertising strategy.

Part of the answer to what role these videos played can be found by comparing these videos to their general election campaign counterparts—the campaign film—to explore the story lines present at the two stages of the campaign. Understanding what dominant story lines exist in the primary videos and campaign films can tell us much about what the campaigns were trying to accomplish at each stage of the race. The primary videos/campaign films are similar in that they represent the longest ad spots that the candidates ran during the primary and general election campaigns. These videos/films, which run between 5 and 20 minutes each, let the candidates advertise their issues and images to voters nationwide in a more comprehensive way than their 30- to 60-second TV ads allowed. This extra length of time gave the campaigns their best opportunity to make their case and connect with voters. Analyzing these videos/films provides for a useful exploration of presidential campaign communication—and packaging—in the 2000 race.

AL GORE'S GENERAL ELECTION CAMPAIGN FILM: HE HAS VALUES

The 11-minute campaign film, which is narrated by Tipper Gore, looks like a video version of a photo album, with many black and white and color photos and handwritten captions under the photos. This intimate style helps the campaign film make its main point: Gore has deep-rooted family values, both in his public and private life. But the campaign film is slightly different from Gore's primary video in that more time is devoted to Gore's values as a husband and father than to his small-town roots.

A Husband and Father

The campaign film opens with a color photo of a young Tipper Gore in a red formal dress. Under the photo is a handwritten caption: "High School, June 10, 1965." In a voice-over, Tipper Gore says: "When I was 16, I met Al at a party after his graduation prom. Remember formal dresses and corsages? We had come with different dates, but wound up hitting it off better with each other. I remember, right from the start, he was a good listener, and he had the most intense and beautiful blue eyes. He called me the next day and soon we began to fall in love." Their love story also is put within the larger social context of the baby boomer generation. With a caption that says "The Late '60s," black and white film footage is shown of Dr. Martin Luther King's 1963 speech at Lincoln Memorial and of police and protesters clashing.

Gore's campaign film frames his service in Vietnam by looking at it through the eyes of his wife. Tipper Gore notes how Gore agonized over his decision to enlist in the military. She also talks about how their first home after getting married was in a trailer park near Ft. Rucker, Alabama, where Gore trained before leaving for Vietnam.

Tipper Gore also recounts their early married years through the values frame. She notes that after their first daughter, Karenna, was born, in 1973, Gore took time off from work to be close to his family. Tipper then talks about how she later returned to work, as a photographer for *The Tennessean*, and got to work alongside her reporter husband.

Gore's 24 years of federal government service is framed as a balancing act between being a public servant and father. Tipper Gore recounts the time young Congressman Gore made a special family request to the Speaker of the House:

Al always worked long hours, but as busy as he was he put his family first. One year I remember Al going to Speaker Tip O'Neill and saying "Sir, you scheduled votes on Halloween night." The speaker just looked back at him. And Al said, "Well, there are a lot of us with kids who want to take them trick-or-treating." The speaker realized how important this was to Al and other young parents in Congress and changed the schedule. With an even busier schedule today, he still manages to make time for Halloween.

The visual imagery used during Tipper Gore's Halloween remarks reinforces the frame of a family-friendly Gore. Included in the campaign film are color snapshots of Gore's children in Halloween costumes and Al Gore made up in green paint to look like Frankenstein.

Another key husband/father moment in the film shows how Gore helped his son recover from a car accident and his wife recover from clinical depression. Tipper Gore notes how their son's accident led to her emotional distress. The visuals shown during her remarks include a photo of Gore sitting with his son in the hospital, then a photo of Tipper, almost in tears, looking away from the camera, then a photo of Al and Tipper laughing together. The final visual in this section of the campaign film, a photo of Al and Tipper at a White House-sponsored conference on mental health, connects Gore's good husband/father images to Gore's government service.

Family Values

Tipper Gore emphasizes how Gore's personal and political values can be traced to his upbringing. She talks about his sister, Nancy, "a beautiful woman with a wit to match," and his mother, Pauline, who was "one of the first women to graduate from Vanderbilt Law School and still one of the wisest women I know." In an effort to make this family values frame connect with women voters, a key Democratic constituency, Tipper Gore adds that Gore's mother and sister were "both strong, intelligent, independent women who, I think, gave Al an early and lasting respect for women and their views." The visual image during Tipper Gore's remarks reinforces this woman-friendly image: an old black and white photo is shown of Gore, his father and mother in a jeep—with his sister at the wheel of the jeep, driving the family.

GEORGE W. BUSH'S GENERAL ELECTION CAMPAIGN FILM: HE HAS VALUES

Bush's nine-minute campaign film, "The Sky's the Limit," in many ways matches the family values and small-town values frames found in Gore's campaign film and primary campaign video. In the same way that Gore uses footage from his rural boyhood home to connote small-town values, Bush's campaign film opens with rural scenes of the candidate walking around on his Texas ranch with his dog. Bush, who wears a blue, open-collar shirt and a white cowboy hat, then talks with one of his ranch hands and stands next to his blue jeep.

Small-Town Values

Bush makes the point that his upbringing in Midland, Texas, gave him values that are still with him. During footage of home movies of Boy Scouts raising an American flag and kids playing baseball, Bush says:

It was the kind of life that I think a lot of Americans feel is slipping away. Safe kids everywhere. Baseball. Barbecues. Football games after church. Midland's out in the middle of nowhere, really. It's kind of on the edge. And I know this may sound trite, but back in the '50s, people who went to Midland were pretty daring and were kind of pioneers, entrepreneurial pioneers in many ways. There used to be a slogan in Midland that said, "The sky's the limit," which is really such an optimistic slogan. It's how I feel about America, really.

Barbara Bush and former President Bush make appearances in the campaign film to validate the small-town values frame. The former president, interviewed at his home, says, "You know, they're the same values that everybody here teaches their own kids: be honest, tell the truth, give somebody else credit." Barbara Bush, also interviewed at home, says, "The kids all were the same. They all went to public schools and then on to high school."

A Son, a Husband, a Father, and a Governor

A wide variety of people, ranging from Bush's mother to a Democratic mayor from Texas, speak about Bush's personal and political qualifications through the values frame. In the film, Barbara Bush shares with viewers how her son helped her cope with feelings of loss after her daughter Robin died from leukemia. George W. Bush also talks about the values he learned from that family traumatizing experience: "It was a tough time. The thing I've come away from that is that marriages face stressful situations and sometimes a stressful situation like that can wreck a marriage. In this case, it made my mother and dad's marriage that much stronger. Brought 'em together and brought our family together." The visuals accompanying Bush's remarks back up the claim that the family is stronger today for the experience. Home movies of the family playing horseshoes at the Bush family home in Kennebunkport, Maine, is shown. The camera moves from George W, who is throwing horseshoes, to former President Bush, to Barbara Bush, who is smiling.

The campaign film then shifts to Laura Bush's love story relationship with her husband. Viewers see home movies of George and Laura's courtship in the 1970s, which Laura Bush calls "a whirlwind romance." Barbara Bush says she was surprised at how quickly he fell in love with her. She notes how Bush first introduced his new girlfriend: "George knocked on the door and he said, 'Mother, I want you to meet Laura Welch. She's the girl I have to marry.' And I said, 'What?' And he meant, ' I'm going to marry.' "

Bush's campaign film uses framing techniques most ably when it tries to downplay—and even turn into a strength—Bush's penchant for verbal gaffes. In one segment of the video, where George and Laura are sitting together outside, Bush talks about how proud he is that his daughters have just graduated from high school. He adds: "And it just seems like yesterday that we were at the hospital have [pause] giving birth." He then laughs with Laura at his verbal gaffe. The campaign film then cuts to Bush, who is riding in his jeep, saying: "I like to laugh. And I like to laugh with people and, uh, you know, sometimes I find myself [pause] I need to laugh at some of the things that I say." By framing Bush's tongue-tied speaking style as just another values moment for Bush, the viewer is inoculated to criticism that Bush is not serious enough to be president.

Bush's campaign film also uses the "values" frame to alter perceptions that Bush's upbringing in a wealthy family has left him out of touch with most Americans. One segment of the film is devoted to telling the story of Bush's volunteer work some years ago in a minority outreach program called PULL (Professionals United Leadership League). Bush notes that the children he helped mentor in Houston "were coming from tough circumstances." This portion of the film provides Bush the opportunity to show the values of serving others, an offshoot of the more formal public service found in politics. Bush also is seen here as being able to empathize and work together with all types of Americans. This sentiment is validated by Ernie Ladd, co-founder of PULL: "We're all made in the image of God, regardless of the color of skin, and George Bush was a part of working for the city of Houston. The city of Houston can be very well thankful for George Bush."

In the same way Gore's campaign film puts the Gores' love story within the larger social context of the baby boomer generation, Bush uses baby boomer imagery and identification to further his frame as a responsible father, husband, and governor. In a voice-over, Bush notes that "one of the great challenges of our generation is to assume responsibility and leadership. We started out as the 'If it feels good, do it' generation." Footage shown during his remarks includes black and white video of hippies dancing in a park. Then color footage is shown of grown-up boomers at work, and a mom driving her kids in her mini-van. Bush continues: "But now we're moms and dads and business leaders and teachers. If we don't help others, if we don't step up and lead, who will? It's one of the reasons I ran for governor of Texas."

Carlos M. Ramirez, the mayor of El Paso, Texas—and a Democrat—appears in the campaign film to give bipartisan validation to the Republican governor's values frame. Ramirez, who is shown in his office, says, "The governor has family values that are very dear to Hispanics. We have seen that. He embraces those family values."

Phyllis Hunter, who is part of a reading program in Texas, then explains how the governor's values apply to public service. She says:

I have seen a big difference since he's been the governor of the state of Texas in the amount of support that we have to help us as educators reach the standards. He said, "If you need it, we'll give it to you." We have Web sites, we have grant programs. We have teacher training in the state of Texas, and we have George leading the way. George W.—people ask me why I have followed him so intently in this education and reading. I've followed him because he's been a leader. He's been leading the way.

CONCLUSIONS AND IMPLICATIONS FOR THE CAMPAIGN FILMS VS. PRIMARY VIDEOS

Frame analysis of the Gore and Bush primary videos and campaign films tells something of how the campaigns wished to package themselves during the two stages of the campaign. In his primary video and general election campaign film, Gore used the "values" frame to distance himself from Washington, D.C., the White House, and President Clinton. Gore wanted to be seen as "his own man," an honorable man with small-town roots, a loving wife, and loving children. Much of the footage in Gore's primary video and campaign film is the same. This similarity at the two stages of the campaign provided the kind of image consistency that political communication scholars argue is useful in presidential campaigning. Devlin (1994) found with the 1992 primary TV ads that candidates who retained a fixed image fared well in comparison with candidates who produced multiple images.

Bush, on the other hand, used one frame for his primary video ("change") and another for his campaign film ("values"). However, Bush's primary video frame was consistent with his other television advertising during the early stage of the primary campaign (Goetzl, 1999). Rather than tell his life story, Bush hoped voters would see him as the best chance the GOP had to change the party and the country. By the time he got the nomination, however, Bush's campaign saw the need to flesh out what kind of a person the candidate was other than being the eldest son of a former president.

The primary videos and campaign films for Gore and Bush tended to be mostly consistent in their verbal and visual messages. These messages, which encompassed a wide variety of biographical and issue information, gravitated toward a single theme for each of the videos/films. This finding adds validation to the study's premise that framing can be a useful tool to explore political advertising.

When one looks at the framing techniques found in all the primary videos and campaign films, one is struck by how useful and efficient it is to employ a single theme to explain vast quantities of personal and political information. Without a unifying theme/frame, viewers would easily get lost trying to understand and interpret a candidate's stand on issues ranging from a strategic missile defense to school vouchers to campaign finance reform. The packaging of personal information also benefits from the use of framing. As was seen with the explanation of McCain's divorce and Bush's speaking gaffes, framing allows political advertisers to inoculate viewers on the candidate's possibly negative attributes.

Framing also lets the primary videos and campaign films accentuate the positive personal attributes of the candidate. Gore, who in reality spent the bulk of his childhood living in a hotel in Washington, D.C., with his senator father, is perhaps the most vivid example of how framing can be used to craft a candidate's image. Gore is framed in both his primary video and campaign film as a small-town boy who, as family friend Jerry Futrell put it, had "a knowledge of the dirt, of the grass roots, of what life was all about."

There is much similarity in style as well as substance between the primary videos and the campaign films. Both typically start off with a brief biographical segment followed by a discussion of key issues that the candidate stands for. Sometimes the frames are different for the biographical and issue segments, but mostly a single frame is used to organize all segments of each primary video/campaign film.

This chapter has begun the process of understanding presidential primary videos by using a qualitative approach to provide answers to this study's main research question: "What function do these videos serve in presidential primary campaigns?"

At this point in the study, it seems clear that these primary videos serve as a cost-effective vehicle to present a massive array of biographical and issue information about their candidate to key voters. Framing techniques, then, are used to organize the up to 20 minutes of information in each video into a single theme that viewers can understand, interpret, and accept.

The next chapter will begin the "triangulation" of methods approach by employing a quantitative method—content analysis—to discover additional meaning in the 2000 presidential primary videos. Many questions still need to be answered about primary videos, including: whether they are "image" or "issue" based, what types of symbolic roles are used to make the candidate appear "presidential," and what locations and types of people are shown to connect the viewer with the candidate and establish identification and legitimacy. These and other questions are best answered in a manifest content analysis—using operational definitions found in a past political communication research—to increase validity of the findings.

Chapter Four

Analyzing Content: Image and Issue Appeals, Archetypal Images, and Presidential Symbolic Roles in the 2000 Campaign Videocassettes

Now that frame analysis has revealed the dominant story lines embedded in the primary videocassettes of the 2000 presidential primary campaign, a manifest content analysis can contribute additional insight in an attempt to answer the study's main research questions.

While research has been done on TV network discourse on political issues, and while political communication scholarship has analyzed the content of presidential campaign TV ads and presidential campaign films, there has been no scholarly, systematic content analysis of presidential primary videocassettes. The content analysis presented in this chapter explores the function of these videos from the perspective of the following:

Issue-based vs. image-based appeals to voters

The archetypal images found in the candidates' primary videos

The symbolic roles the candidates present themselves in to voters

The types of locations and people shown in the videos to display diversity and identify the candidate with different parts of the country.

THE INFLUENCE OF IMAGES AND ISSUES

Research has found that campaign ads are useful to study because the spots can substantially affect the candidate's image in the viewer's mind (Cundy, 1986, 1990; Kahn and Greer, 1994; Kaid, 1997; Scammell, 1990). Also, while campaign ads may address few issues, the information they do provide is absorbed by viewers (Just, Crigler and Wallach, 1990).

Much academic research has been done on campaign TV advertising to understand whether political spots mostly convey pleasing images of the candidate to viewers or whether the ads inform voters of the issues. Garramone (1986) looked at how TV political ads can create a favorable candidate image with voters. She classifies political ads as either "issue" or "image" ads. Issue ads have certain distinct characteristics: They spend more time outlining the candidate's policy stands, show the candidate speaking directly to voters in a "talking head ad," use simpler production techniques, and use language that is more specific. Image ads, on the other hand: spend more time playing up the candidate's personal qualities, show the candidate in action with family or supporters, use more complex production techniques, and use language that is more general, which allows for more inferences to be made by the viewer. Other researchers looking at image and issue ads have used similar definitions (Kaid and Sanders, 1978; Joslyn, 1980, 1986; Shyles, 1984, 1986; Thorson, Christ, and Caywood, 1991; Chanslor, 1995; Kaid, Chanlor and Hovind, 1992).

Joslyn (1980) found most presidential ads—more than 70%—mentioned issues between 1960 and 1976. He argued, "Political spot ads may not be as poor a source of information as many observers have claimed." Shyles (1986), too, rejected the view that all political commercials contain more personality and character information than issue information (p. 97). But in 1986, Joslyn content analyzed 506 political TV ads (from presidential campaigns to U.S. House races) from 1960 to 1984 and found that while issues are mentioned, only 5% of the 506 ads had specific policy preferences. Ads that had only vague or ambiguous policy references dominated in the sample. He found that 40% of the ads were "ritualistic" in that they "articulate cultural myth or values with which few are likely to disagree, [they are] commercials which rely upon the symbols of a political community, and commercials which are melodramas" (p. 173).

Research shows that issue ads can have a powerful effect on voters. Kaid and Sanders (1978) found that candidates can achieve higher evaluations among voters when they present issue information in their ads. Thorson, Christ, and Caywood (1991) found that "issue commercials produced greater voting intent, and more positive attitudes toward the ads, the candidates, their abilities, and their characters" (p. 480). So while issues can be found (and can be useful to the candidates) in campaign TV ads, the question remains whether the same is true for primary campaign videos. The present study attempts to answer this question.

THE ARCHETYPAL IMAGES IN CAMPAIGN FILMS

Morreale argues that certain archetypal images run through most presidential campaign films, which are the closest political cousin to primary campaign videocassettes. While she did not number them, the rhetorical and visual patterns can be categorized to include the following:

Candidates learn responsibility and love of country from their father, while learning religious and other core moral values from their mother.

Candidates have a hard-scrabble beginning in life, but succeed through hard work.

Candidates have a "love story" relationship with their spouse.

Candidates are good with their children and/or grandchildren.

Candidates come from "small-town America."

Candidates are athletic.

The candidate is a modern Cincinnatus, concerned foremost with duty to country.

Candidates display wartime heroism.

Candidates are associated with political party heroes of the past.

Candidates have the power to restore the "American Dream" that has been temporarily lost. (pp. 6–14)

Morreale (1994b) also found a key difference between Democratic and Republican campaign strategies. While Democrats have historically focused their campaign energies on promoting their candidate, Republicans have taken a broader approach, honing their niche marketing skills. These differences were reflected in the two parties' campaign films:

Until recently, the audience-oriented Republicans projected images and evoked myths that addressed deep-seated yearnings, while the candidate-centered Democrats reflected images of the candidate with little regard for the hopes and desires that fueled the American psyche. The Republicans, fluent in the language of television, provided visual and verbal messages that supported one another and bound their constituencies, while the Democrats often undercut verbal messages with incongruent visual forms and images. (p. 38)

But, as Morreale writes, in the 1992 campaign Bill Clinton and his team learned from Democratic mistakes of the past and embraced the Republican strategy for making campaign films (p. 36).

The handful of other academic studies of presidential campaign films examined more specialized aspects of the medium. Novak (1995) examined the character and leadership association campaign films that George Bush and Clinton tried to create in the minds of voters in 1992. Novak (1997) then compared Clinton's 1992 and 1996 general election campaign films and found much similarity between the two films in rhetoric, symbolism, and ritual. Wye (1996) explored John F. Kennedy's 1960 campaign film efforts to show the extent to which a candidate will go to shape his or her public image. Morreale (1991) analyzed the documentary style used in Ronald Reagan's 1984 campaign film, and how Reagan's political advertising team inaugurated the rebirth of mythology in campaigning.

THE IMPORTANCE OF SYMBOLISM IN POLITICAL COMMUNICATION

Friedman (1973) examined what qualities make political leaders and institutions "legitimate" and possessing "authority." He argues that political institutions are said to have "authority" or "legitimacy" to the extent to which the members of society regard those institutions as reflecting, embodying, or promoting their shared beliefs. He adds that political scientists historically have noted that "authority" in people is denoted by certain "marks," or "signs" or "symbols." According to Friedman, "Many different things have been viewed by human beings as 'marks' of authority: office, social station, property, 'great' power, pedigree, religious claims, 'miracles,' etc.... The concept of authority can thus have an application only within the context of certain socially accepted criteria which serve to identify the person(s) whose utterances are to count as authoritative" (pp. 133–134).

In modern political advertising, these "marks" or "symbols" are reflected in the candidates' TV spot ads. Kaid and Davidson (1986) examined political TV ads for verbal and nonverbal content and for film/video production techniques. They note: "When candidates use television to project themselves to voters, they engage primarily in a form of pseudo interpersonal communication in which they use television's visual element and its capacity to induce intimacy to portray themselves as they believe voters wish to see them. Their methods of self-portrayal make up their videostyles" (p.185).

Along these lines, Kaid and Davidson found differences between challengers and incumbents in their videostyles. Incumbents used longer commercials, more testimonials, a more candidate-positive focus, and more slides with print; dressed more formally; had an announcer doing a voice-over; and verbally and visually stressed "competence" (p. 199). Challengers used a more opposition-negative focus and a more cinéma vérité style, showed "head-one" shots of the candidate, used more eye contact between camera and audience, dressed more casually, spoke for self more, and had fewer surrogate speakers (p. 199). While these findings may be true for a challenger's TV spot ads, the question remains whether these findings can be generalized to presidential primary videos, which are used only by challengers.

Graber (1987) holds that the words a candidate uses contain the richest source of marks and symbols: "Words are like Pavlovian cues—just as animals can be taught to associate the sound of a bell with food—so people are continually conditioned to associate verbal cues with past direct and vicarious experiences. Verbal conditioning can be done most effectively through what political linguists call condensation symbols. These are more popularly called code words. Examples are "the American way," "racism," "special interests," "rainbow coalition," and, yes, "where's the beef?" (p. 185).

Graber argues that there are five functions of political language: (1) create a reality that is favorable to the candidate; (2) reconstruct the past and predict the future; (3) interpret and link a candidate with positive or negative symbols (for example, stimulus generalization is the idea that if a candidate is good at one activity, he must be good in another, even if it is only remotely related); (4) set the agenda of the campaign; and (5) stimulate action on the part of citizens to vote and/or contribute time and money to the candidate.

Nimmo (1987) continues this symbolic line of thinking when he notes that presidential election campaigns are "a continuous exercise in the creation, re-creation, and transmission of significant symbols through language, both verbal and nonverbal" (p. 159). In defining the word "symbol," he writes: "A symbol is simply a work, action, or picture (hence is verbal or nonverbal) that designates an idea, object, event, etc." (p. 160). He adds that candidates seek significant symbols, those that will elicit from voters the response sought by the candidate. "In this respect, campaign appeals are efforts at manipulating symbols in order to create shared, sympathetic responses" (p. 160).

Nimmo adds that symbols are used as part of the ritual of political campaigning. He defines rituals as a "series of acts that are regularly and faithfully performed or that recur in a patterned way; the acts are repeated time and time again with minimal variations" (p. 165). Examples of rituals include religious or inauguration ceremonies and even sports rituals such as the coin toss at the start of a football game. He adds: "Ritual dramas permit actors to demonstrate that they are doing something familiar, legitimate, acceptable, valid, or socially/morally approved" (p. 165). Certain phrases and actions can be ritualistic, such as when a candidate "runs on the issues." Certain words tend to be used constantly, such as "change" and "new." He says that words such as these evoke certain emotions in people, but the words are also sufficiently vague so as to give the candidate wiggle room as to their exact meanings (p. 169). Certain media coverage can be ritualistic, such as how a "front runner" or a "dark horse" is covered.

A WAY TO OPERATIONALIZE PRESIDENTIAL SYMBOLIC ROLES

Roberts (1993) explored presidential TV spots from 1952 to 1988 and found 10 presidential symbolic roles that candidates have emitted in their ads to conform to the public's image of a president:

The Great Communicator

Chief Visionary

Hero

Father Figure
Chief Budget Setter
Official Keeper of American Values
Commander-in-Chief
Chief Legislator
World Leader
Chief Educator

She found that presidential campaign commercials from 1952 to 1988 visually and verbally emphasized several of these symbolic roles: "great communicator," "chief budget setter," "chief visionary" and "official keeper of American values" (p. 12). Her operationalization of these terms includes "great communicator" (gives a speech, press conference, talks with voters), "chief visionary" (talks about the future, dream, destiny, space), "hero" (large crowds cheering, working late in office, war hero, medals, honors), "father figure" (with children, with family, photos of family in office), "chief budget setter" (talks about economy, taxes, inflation, prices, welfare), "official keeper of American values" (mentions rights, freedom, equality, peace), "commander-in-chief" (seen with armed forces, domestic riots, law enforcement), "chief legislator" (addresses Congress, meets congressional leaders, proposes bill), "world leader" (seen with foreign leaders, signing treaties, talks about world peace), and "chief educator" (appears as a role model in an educational/training situation). Roberts argues that a successful presidential candidate tries to fit into as many of these roles as possible: "Just as the tailor tries on the various pieces of cloth for measurement and fit, the campaign period allows the presidential candidates an opportunity to model the various roles for fit and acceptability before the American public" (p. 7).

This study on presidential primary videos builds on the existing knowledge of political myths, symbols, and rituals and uses Roberts's operationalization of the term "presidential symbolic roles" as the basis to explore the symbolic function of primary videos.

THE IMPORTANCE OF SETTING AND LOCATION IN POLITICAL COMMUNICATION

The presidential primary video is part of a candidate's broad appeal to voters. Who is seen in the videos can be useful to study because it gives us an idea of the audience to whom the candidate is reaching out. Faucheux (1994) notes a key question to answer in political advertising: "From a geographic, ethnic, partisan, social, and demographic perspective, will this message appeal to the groups necessary for my winning coalition?" (p. 49).

In a qualitative analysis of about a thousand presidential general election commercials from 1952 to 1996, Sherr (1999) found that children are a demographic that plays a major role in presidential advertising. Children are displayed symbolically to show economic security, poverty, crime, war, and hope for the future. Images of children in poverty are found far more in ads from the 1960s (they disappeared from ads by the 1970s), while appeals to economic insecurity are used consistently over time. Sherr adds that TV spots involving children consistently featured women, even though their social roles have evolved over time:

By presenting [viewers] with images of healthy children learning, interacting with their families, and experiencing American rituals, politicians assure voters that, under their leadership, the country will continue to flourish. Images of children pledging allegiance to the flag, playing in bucolic natural environments, and waving to visiting politicians act as emotional triggers to elicit feelings of patriotic senti- mentality and optimism that can be carried over to the sponsoring candidate. (p. 57)

What locations are used in political advertising also can have an impact on the image viewers have of the candidate. Edelman (1976) makes the point that settings have "a vital bearing" on the evocation of feeling and aesthetic reactions and add to how "legitimate" voters see the candidate. He argues that "settings have a vital bearing upon actors, upon responses to acts, and especially upon the evocation of feeling and aesthetic reac- tions" (p. 349). He continues, noting that people who witness political acts are likely to take the settings for the act, a building or a particular room, for example, into consideration when judging the legitimacy of the acts. One example he gives is that a setting deemed completely appropriate for selling groceries would be completely inappropriate for conducting the business of state. Exploring the settings and types of people found in pres- idential primary videos could be helpful in understanding if the videos provide a legitimizing function for the candidates.

CONTENT ANALYSIS OF THE 2000 PRIMARY CAMPAIGN VIDEOCASSETTES

Content analysis addresses the following five research areas:

Q1 Are the videos primarily issue-based, image-based, or balanced between image and issue appeals?

Q2 Which of Morreale's campaign film archetypal images are found in the can- didates' primary videos?

Q3 Which of Roberts's TV spot ad presidential symbolic roles are seen and heard in these videos?

Q4 How broad/narrow is the spectrum of locations used in the videos?

Q5 How broad/narrow is the spectrum of people shown in the videos?

In addition, this coding scheme was applied to the two campaign films of the 2000 race to understand the differences between the messages found in these two unique types of political communication.

Two researchers, both trained in content analysis, coded for the presence or absence (visually and/or verbally) of Morreale's (1993) archetypal images and Roberts's (1993) presidential symbolic roles. "Image" vs. "issue" appeals were coded based on Garramone's (1986) definition. The locations seen in the videos were coded as follows: unidentifiable office, Oval Office, the candidate's official office (such as congressional or governor), military setting, foreign country, classroom, industrial, athletic, home, rally, urban, rural, outside Congress, inside House or Senate, and other. The people seen in the videos were coded as follows: children, senior citizens, African Americans, Hispanics, Asians, disabled, veterans, women, blue-collar workers, white-collar workers, member(s) of the candidate's family, and other.

The two coders coded 100% of the primary videos and campaign films. Inter-coder reliability, which was tested using Holsti's formula, was 97% (Holsti, 1969). Because the research examines the universe of videos under study, a census, or tests of significance are unnecessary (Stempel, 1981; Riffe, Lacy and Fico, 1998). See Appendix A for a copy of the code sheet used.

"IMAGE" APPEALS VS. "ISSUE" APPEALS

One of the key findings from examining primary campaign videos is that while past political communication research has found the 30-second TV ad spots of politicians to be wanting in terms of issues and substance, presidential primary videos stand out as issue-rich. The primary videos of Gary Bauer and Bill Bradley were classified as "primarily issue-based," while the videos of George W. Bush, John McCain, and Steve Forbes were classified as "truly balanced between image and issue appeals." Only Al Gore's video was classified as "primarily image-based."

Bauer's primary campaign video, titled "Who I am and What I Believe," embodies the issue-based approach. Bauer argues in depth his position on many hotly debated issues such as a tax reform, a ballistic missile defense system, medical savings accounts, school vouchers, and a return to a Reagan administration requirement that all federal agencies release "family impact statements" on new government regulations. He also details his opposition on issues such as the current favorable trade status between the United States and China, expanded rights for gays, and abortion.

On the issue of tax reform, Bauer talks about how a $500 per child tax credit benefits working families. He also is shown on *Meet the Press*, promising a 16% across-the-board, flat federal income tax rate if he makes it to the White House and challenging his Republican rivals to match his plan: "I'm going to stand strongly for the idea that that money ought to be returned to the business people, the entrepreneurs, the investors, the American family that are responsible for that surplus. And I believe that my 16% rate is, in fact, the lowest rate of any flat tax on the table, and I'm looking forward to debating Steve Forbes and others about this."

On social issues, Bauer's video goes beyond vague talk of "family values" to address several controversial policy stands. Bauer's opposition to legalizing gay marriage is explained by telling the story of a confrontation he had recently with gay-rights activists while speaking at an event at Harvard University. Bauer says that what he experienced at the Harvard event, which was covered by C-Span, was "a perfect little snapshot of the great debate I think we're going to have in America as we go into the next century about the place of morality in public policy." Then C-Span footage of the event shows Bauer being called a "Nazi" and a persecutor of gays by one member of the audience and asked if his "vision of American foreign policy" includes "bigotry and hatred spreading around the world." The primary video then cuts to Bauer back in his office, talking about how he replied to the charges: "I confronted those students when I said that when they come into the public square and try to change the definition of marriage to be two men or two women, or when they insist that the Boy Scouts and the Salvation Army has to change their rules and regulations to accommodate the demands of the gay rights movement. When I stood up to those questions, the audience— even at liberal Harvard—applauded."

On the Democratic side of the campaign, Bill Bradley's primary videocassette, titled "People Are Talking," also mostly focuses on issues, though Bradley is not the one doing the talking. Rather, it is TV commentators ranging from CNN political analyst Bill Schneider to NBC political analyst Tim Russert, who speak about issues revolving around Bradley's electability. Another issue, that of campaign finance reform, is addressed by Minnesota senator Paul Wellstone.

The three primary campaign videos to be classified as "truly balanced between image and issue appeals" (Bush, Forbes, and McCain) also covered a wide range of public policy issues. George W. Bush's video, titled "Fresh Start," stresses issues such as employment growth, juvenile crime reduction, government spending, tort reform, and educational reform. Bush spends the most time outlining his education initiatives, which include a rigorous testing program for students and schools: "I believe in high standards and high expectations. I believe holding people accountable for results. We measure, we post the results, we blow the whistle on failure. And if any child falls down, we make sure they get extra help before we give up. Education is vital. Because there are no second-rate children, and no second-rate dreams."

The image-based portion of Bush's video shows Bush as likable and comfortable with many types of people and many types of situations. In one scene, Bush is in a diner pouring coffee for the customers. A clip from *The New York Times* shown during this footage notes that Bush is "a personable and charismatic campaigner." Later, Bush and his wife Laura walk up to a suburban lemonade stand being run by two young girls. Bush pays and gets some pink lemonade. The couple drink as reporters in the background cover the photo-op.

Steve Forbes's video, titled "A Rebirth of Freedom," argues in favor of many issues such as medical savings accounts, privatizing Social Security, school vouchers, and a flat tax. Forbes gives the most detail on his flat tax plan, which he says is simpler and fairer than the current federal tax code. A family from Exeter, New Hampshire—the Daley family—is presented in the video to personalize how tax code changes can impact peoples' lives. Forbes notes that the family, which is "struggling" to raise three children, runs a fish market in town and tries to make economic ends meet. Then, while footage is shown of the father preparing lobster in the store, the father says, "I see the flat tax as a viable solution for a person like myself. I think we had it figured out to close to $6,000 in savings."

Forbes's image-based moments can be found mostly during the first half of his video, when Forbes's biographical information is presented. In one segment, Forbes talks about how his interest in politics started many years ago due to his father's political ambitions.

Images and issues tend to be mixed seamlessly in many of the videos. John McCain's video addresses issues such as eliminating the inheritance tax and the so-called marriage penalty, which results from a quirk in the tax code that makes many married couples pay more in taxes than they would if they filed separately. McCain's video, titled "The Character to Do What's Right, the Courage to Fight for It," also speaks in favor of Internet filtering technology and campaign finance reform. On the issue of decreasing the federal government's role in education, the video's narrator notes that McCain "wants federal education dollars sent directly to local school districts so parent and teachers, not Washington bureaucrats, can decide how to best strengthen our schools."

Imagery in McCain's video centers around his character-building experience during the Vietnam War and his relationship with his family. These two elements come together in one portion of the video when McCain talks about his family homecoming after returning from more than five years in a prisoner of war camp: "During my absence in Vietnam, there was a large number of pets of all kinds that were kept in our house. And my daughter, Sidney, was six months old when I left to go to Vietnam and was six years old when I returned. So when my wife, Carol, was telling her, 'Your Daddy's coming home,' she said, 'Oh, yea? And where will he sleep and what do we feed him?'"

Even Gore's video, which is classified as "primarily image-based," touches on issues such as Social Security, arms control, the environment, and educational reform. But his video, titled "The Al Gore Story," fails to provide any depth on these issues. Gore's comments on educational reform, made to a crowd in Bedford, New Hampshire, demonstrates the lack of an issue-based appeal: "The number one priority, in my opinion, is to bring about truly revolutionary change in public education. And I would say that anyone who does not want a president who takes the oath of office and sets about revolutionary changes in education, if that's not what they want, then don't vote for me. But if that is what you want, then I ask for your support." No specifics are laid out by the vice president as to what kind of "revolutionary" changes he is talking about. This kind of vague language is consistent with what Joslyn (1986) called "ritualistic" appeals in that it can only "articulate cultural myths or values with which few are likely to disagree" (pp. 139–183). Gore sidestepped any talk of policies or programs. He never attempted to take credit for the economic recovery that happened under the watch of his administration. There are no references to the economic turnaround, including decreasing unemployment, decreasing deficit numbers, and rising wages.

The finding that primary campaign videos tend to have a high level of issue-orientation to them adds to the significance of the videos as a form of political communication. These videos are not merely "slobberfests," as Mundy (1995) called them. Rather, these videos provide a wealth of complex issue information to help educate and persuade viewers on key issues of the day. At the same time, most of the videos also supply a healthy dose of image-based information to help show the candidates as not only "right" on the issues, but as likable family men whom voters would be proud to call their president.

This discovery is quite different from the findings for the general election campaign films of Gore and Bush. Both films are classified as "primarily image-based." In fact, no public policy issues are addressed in any detail in either film; the films merely play up the strong values the candidates say they have. When the candidates talk about politics, which is not often, the words and phases used are best described—as Joslyn put it—as "ritualistic." In Gore's campaign film, Gore talks vaguely about the need to "make democracy work the way it's supposed to." Later, he adds: "We have to accept responsibility for choosing the destiny of America."

Bush's campaign film is equally lacking in issue content. In one scene, Bush is shown in a classroom speaking to a group of African-American children. He reads a letter that they wrote for him: "Dear Governor Bush. Thank you for coming to our school and for your visit. Thank you for trying to be our president. We hope that a lot of people vote for you." Then Bush says to them: "So do I." They laugh. He continues: "If you become president, we hope that you will make the world safer and that there will be no more bad guys."

These phrases are ritualistic because few would disagree with Gore's call to "make democracy work" or Bush's desire to "make the world safer." Compare these platitudes with the serious issue arguments made for campaign finance reform, educational testing, pro-life policies, and tax reform by McCain, Bradley, Bush, Bauer, and Forbes in their primary videos.

This finding makes sense when one considers that the campaign films' dominant frames, which revolve around the theme of family values, do not really dovetail easily with talk of current legislation on Capitol Hill. Also it is important to make a distinction between the audience for the primary video and the campaign film. The campaign film is shown during the general election to a mass audience of millions. The primary video is shown during the primary to a target number of regular voting party faithful who may number 50,000 to 200,000. Seen from this perspective, it is not surprising that most of the primary videos contained many issue arguments. After all, the primary candidates are dealing with voters who are highly and regularly involved in the political process. These voters take the time to research a wide variety of issues. Also, because primary campaigns are intra-party contests, playing up issue differences helps voters differentiate between a host of candidates who at first blush may not seem that different from each other.

MORREALE'S PRESIDENTIAL CAMPAIGN FILM ARCHETYPES

Despite the differences between primary videos and campaign films when it comes to issue content, the videos share many of the archetypes Morreale found with presidential campaign films during the past 50 years [see Table 1]. More than two-thirds of the primary videos displayed the candidate as learning values from parents, being good with their children, being athletic, having duty to their country, associating themselves with past party leaders, and having the power to restore the "American dream."

The theme that the candidate learns responsibility, love of country, and other core values from their parents can be seen in the primary videos of Gore, Bauer, Forbes, and McCain. In Gore's video, Jerry Futrell, a family friend, says that Gore's father went out of his way to make sure that his son "had a knowledge of the dirt, of the grass roots of what life was all about." The narrator in Bauer's video notes that Bauer's father was "an ex-marine who worked long hours in the steel mills, yet he always found

Table 1.
Characteristics of the Candidates on Morreale's Archetypes

	Bill Bradley	Al Gore	Gary Bauer	George W. Bush	Steve Forbes	John McCain	Gore's campaign film	Bush's campaign film
Learns from parents		X	X		X	X	X	X
Has a hard-scrabble beginning		X	X					
Has a love story spouse relationship		X		X		X	X	X
Good with children or grandchildren		X	X		X	X	X	X
Comes from small-town America		X	X				X	X
Is athletic	X	X		X		X	X	X
Is a modern Cincinnatus		X	X		X	X	X	X
Displays wartime heroism		X				X	X	
Associated with past party heroes			X	X	X	X	X	X
Power to restore American dream	X		X	X	X	X		X

time to teach his son life's most important lessons." Bauer says these lessons included the value of studying hard in school: "He used to come home every night, covered with dirt and grime. And the first thing he would do is come to my room and tell me to look at him and then tell me to remember that this is the way he looked when he came home from work, and that I should study and work hard if I wanted to get a better life for myself."

In Forbes's video, one of Forbes's brothers stresses that their parents were strict on teaching values such as how to treat other people. McCain's video links McCain to the values of "duty, honor, and country" that his navy officer father and grandfather embraced.

Four of the six primary videos also showed the candidate as being good with their children. Photos and video footage show Gore with his four children. His eldest daughter, Karenna, also says good things about Gore as a father. In Forbes's video, his daughters also praise the way their father raised them. McCain's video uses the story of how the couple came to adopt their daughter, Bridget, to show McCain as a warm father. In Bauer's video, Bauer talks about the devotion he has to his children despite the time constraints due to his public life: "When I'm trailing around the country and I get back to a hotel room and my head hits the pillow and I turn the lights out, I'm thinking of the love of my wife Carol, what it's going to sound like when I get home the next day and I open the front door and the first words I'm going to hear are my son Zach yelling, 'Dad, let's wrestle.' Or what my daughter looked like when she went out on her first date. Or for that matter, what I looked like when she went out on her first date."

The athleticism archetype is displayed by Bradley, Gore, Bush, and McCain. Gore is seen paddling a canoe with his wife and running the Marine Corps Marathon with his daughters. Old footage in Bradley's video shows him during his days playing basketball for the New York Knicks. Bush's previous job running the Texas Rangers baseball team is alluded to in his video. For McCain, his heroics as a jet fighter pilot during Vietnam are portrayed as athletic.

The Cincinnatus legend of ancient Rome, which speaks of duty to country without expectation of reward, also dominates the primary campaign videos of America's presidential hopefuls. Gore's "Cincinnatus" moment comes when family friends note that Gore volunteered for duty in Vietnam because if he didn't go, somebody else from his hometown would have to go in his place, so he did "what's expected of me." Devotion to duty during Vietnam also plays prominently in McCain's video. The video's narrator reminds viewers that after McCain became a prisoner of war, he had the opportunity for early release because his father was a top-ranking navy officer. But, says the narrator, "McCain repeatedly refused early release, citing the code of conduct that prisoners should be released in the order in which they were captured." The narrator notes that his sense of duty came at a terrible personal price: "For his repeated defiance, his Communist captors savagely beat him." The narrator adds that McCain has "always put America's interests ahead of his own."

The sense of duty displayed by Bauer and Forbes is less dramatic and life threatening. The narrator in Bauer's video explains that at the end of the Reagan administration, Bauer could have cashed in on his high-level executive branch experience by joining a prestigious law firm. Instead, he continued his fight for the causes he believed were right for the country.

In associating themselves with past political leaders, Bauer, Forbes, and McCain link their personality and policies with Ronald Reagan, while former President Bush briefly appears in his son's video, waving to a crowd of supporters. George W. then puts his arm around his father, physically connecting himself to the former president and demonstrating that his famous family's political destiny has been passed to him. Bauer's video makes the most use of his association with Ronald Reagan, which makes sense given that frame analysis of Bauer's video revealed that the dominant story line for the video was that he would "reclaim Reagan's legacy."

McCain's video links the Arizona senator's character to that of Reagan and former Arizona senator Barry Goldwater. In a segment of the video when the narrator says that Americans are looking for a presidential candidate who will "restore integrity to the office," footage from the 1980s is shown of McCain and President Reagan shaking hands. Later, the narrator in McCain's video notes that after McCain succeeded to Goldwater's Senate seat in 1986, he set out to "continue Goldwater's tradition of plaintalk conservatism." Forbes is seen with past foreign leaders, such as Margaret Thatcher, as well as Reagan.

Of all Morreale's archetypes, the "power to restore the American dream" shows up in the most primary videos; all but Gore's video presents this archetype. Each presidential contender found his own way to show he has the power to restore his definition of the "American Dream." Bush promises to "usher in what I call 'the responsibility era'" and "rally the armies of compassion" to make America a better—not just a more prosperous—place to live. Bradley says he wants "the American dream at last." In Forbes's video, his brother Kip uses his family's rags-to-riches history to show that his brother understands the American dream. At the end of McCain's video, the candidate directly addresses the camera to talk about rekindling the American ideal of freedom. He then tells his viewers: "I know that with your help, and others like you, we can win the presidential nomination, carry our message to the American people and begin to restore the American dream."

Bauer spends the most time listing the many ways the American dream has been damaged and how he can help restore the country morally:

I'd like to see a country where reliable standards of right and wrong mattered again. Where character counted, where virtue was seen as something that wasn't hopelessly old fashioned, but something we thought we could pass on from one generation to another. That has had an impact on the American people. I still have enough confidence in average Americans to believe we can pull back from this. That we can get back to a core center of reliable standards of right and wrong.

Half of the primary videos displayed the candidate archetype of the "love story" spouse relationship. Candidates and their wives are seen canoeing together (Gore), laughing together (Bush), and raising their children together (McCain). As was mentioned in chapter 3, frame analysis of Gore's video revealed that the dominant story line for the vice president was his strong values, including his values as a husband.

The final three Morreale archetypes—the candidate having a hard-scrabble start in life, coming from "small-town America," and displaying wartime heroism—were seen in just two of six videos. The Gore and Bauer videos show their candidates as having both a hard-scrabble and small-town American background. The narrator in Bauer's video notes that the Republican hopeful grew up in Newport, Kentucky, with "a blue-collar family." The narrator continues: "Both of his parents were forced to drop out of school during the Great Depression and struggled to provide for their young family." Photos of Newport, which include an old church and a quiet main street area, add to the small-town feel. Interestingly, Gore's video, which is framed in the small-town values motif, argues that this U.S. senator's son, who attended private school in the nation's capital, was actually a small-town boy who had "a knowledge of the dirt, of the grass roots" and worked his way to the top.

Wartime "heroism" is displayed by Gore and McCain, though the archetype fits most easily with McCain's jet fighter and prisoner of war experience in Vietnam. One of many wartime heroism moments comes when the video's narrator recounts how a young Lt. Commander McCain dealt with a fire aboard the aircraft carrier *Forrestal:* "In the ensuing explosions and fire, McCain escaped by crawling onto the nose of his plane and diving into the fire on the ship's deck. He turned to help a fellow pilot, only to be blown back 10 feet when more bombs exploded." Gore's wartime experience was less life threatening. He was a military journalist. Says Gore: "I carried an M-16 and a pencil."

As one might expect, the presidential campaign films of Gore and Bush displayed a far higher percentage of Morreale's campaign film archetypes (80%) than did the six primary videos (57%). Just as in his primary video, Gore's campaign film failed to show the candidate as having the power to restore the American dream. Just as in his primary video, Bush's campaign film neglected any reference of wartime service. The only other missing archetype, which was true for both Gore's and Bush's campaign films, was the "hard-scrabble" upbringing theme.

Bush's campaign film exhibited many more archetypes than the candidate's primary video. Most of the additional archetypes reflect the shift in frames found in Bush's video vs. film. Bush's primary video frame—that he was a "change" for the GOP and the nation—virtually ignored Bush's personal history prior to becoming governor of Texas. But with the visual and verbal messages in Bush's campaign film revolving around the "values" frame, it is not surprising that the film adds in Morreale's archetypes of learning values from parents, coming from small-town America, being good with his children, and having duty to country. While Bush's parents are seen briefly but not heard in the primary video, both of Bush's parents have speaking roles in the campaign film, which highlights the values their son learned as a youngster. Former President Bush notes that his son has "the same values that everybody here teaches their own kids: be honest, tell the truth, give somebody else credit."

In Bush's film, Midland, Texas, is romanticized as the quintessential small town in which to learn strong values. Bush also gets to show himself as a caring and devoted father. While talking about the birth of his twin daughters, Bush says, "It was a great moment when they were born. And I was in the delivery room, and it was just an incredible feeling of life and the preciousness of life."

Interestingly, the only archetype Gore has in his campaign film that is lacking in his primary video is his association with past party leaders. In this case, the past party leader is Republican: Ronald Reagan. This could be seen as an attempt to reach out to so-called Reagan Democrats. The lack of difference in archetypes between Gore's video and film can be attributed to the lack of difference found between the dominant frames found in Gore's video and film. In both cases, Gore used a "values" frame. Furthermore, Morreale's archetypes seem to be more image-oriented, and Gore's video and film reflect this.

Looking back over Morreale's campaign film archetypes, it is clear that the primary videocassettes display much the same imagery as the campaign films. But when this information is combined with the findings from the previous section that examined "image" vs. "issue" appeals, we learn much more. Primary videos also contain abundant amounts of issue information, which campaign films fail to offer.

Part of the reason for these differences may result from the types of voters who turn out for primaries versus the general election. Research from the 1950s through the 1980s reveals that primary voters for both major political parties tend to be older, more educated, and more politically aware than general election voters (Key, 1956; Ranney 1972, 1977; Bartels 1988). These voters may be more accepting of issue-based appeals and may even demand that they get "the straight talk" on issues from the candidates.

ROBERTS'S PRESIDENTIAL SYMBOLIC ROLES

While Roberts found "great communicator," "chief budget setter," "chief visionary" and "official keeper of American values" as the most used symbolic roles in presidential TV spot ads since the 1950s, the most used symbolic roles in the presidential primary videos were "great communicator," "chief visionary," and "father figure" [see Table 2].

While all primary videocassettes presented these three symbols, each candidate had a unique way of trying on these roles. For the "great communicator" role, Gore takes advantage of the perks of being vice president by being shown in his video speaking at an event on the lawn of the White House. Symbolically, the vice president looks as if he has already assumed the presidency. He also speaks to crowds in Tennessee. Bradley's video be-

Table 2.
Characteristics of the Candidates on Roberts' Symbolic Roles

	Bill Bradley	Al Gore	Gary Bauer	George W. Bush	Steve Forbes	John McCain	Gore's campaign film	Bush's campaign film
The great communicator	X	X	X	X	X	X	X	X
Chief visionary	X	X	X	X	X	X	X	X
Heroic	X		X	X	X	X	X	X
Father figure	X	X	X	X	X	X	X	X
Chief budget setter			X	X	X	X		
Official keeper of American values	X		X	X	X	X	X	X
Commander-in-chief		X	X	X		X	X	
Chief legislator						X	X	
World leader					X		X	
Chief educator		X	X	X	X		X	X

gins and ends with CNN coverage of the candidate giving his presidential announcement speech to a large gathering in Crystal City, Missouri. At the end of his speech, Bradley also shows his nonverbal communication skills by using a sweeping hand motion to command the crowd to rise. He then says, "Come with me."

The last third of Bush's video is devoted to a single presidential campaign speech that the Texas governor gave to a crowd in the Midwest. Bush uses this setting to spell out his major issue stands. Forbes shows his communication skills by speaking from the pulpit of an African-American church. McCain's video includes several scenes of the senator meeting voters, including one where McCain is shaking hands and talking with voters in a town square in an unidentified location. Toward the end of Bauer's video, the candidate talks about family values to an audience in an unidentified auditorium: "Believe in those things, stand for those things, fight for those things, teach your family about those things."

The "chief visionary" role also is tailored to fit the candidate. Sometimes the candidate's vision is validated with testimonials, such as in Gore's video. Toward the end of the video, Tennessee teacher Eleanor Smotherman speaks well of the vision of her former student: "We've heard where there's no vision, the people perish. I believe he's had a vision of the great need to prepare himself for service for people, not only in our community but in our nation."

The narrator in McCain's video also substantiates the vision of the senator and war hero: "He's a man more tested and better prepared than anyone to lead America into the twenty-first century." In Forbes's primary video, Bob Forbes authenticates his brother Steve's vision, saying Steve is "passionate about issues in the country that deal with human potential."

In the videos of Bush, Bauer, and Bradley, the candidates speak to their vision. Bush talks about his vision for the future to a midwestern crowd. He says, "We will give this great land called America a fresh start after a season of cynicism." Bauer and Bradley also speak in broad terms about their general philosophical vision for America.

The "father figure" role is displayed in a fairly universal style. For the most part, the candidate is shown as a loving father to his own children and a strong but friendly figure to other children. Gore's video uses this role extensively. Not only does his wife and eldest daughter validate his fatherly qualities, Gore talks to a crowd about the joys of being a new grandfather: "Tipper and I are expecting our first grandchild at the end of June. And I've been getting some advice, and I'm just glad to find out that you don't have to look old to be a granddad."

Bush's video has many scenes where the candidate is seen hugging, laughing, poking fun with, and generally being a good influence on children from various ethnic and racial backgrounds. In one segment, while Bush is seen shaking hands with smiling Hispanic children, a quote from *The Midland Reporter-Telegram* newspaper is superimposed on the screen: "He's promoting the need to teach abstinence."

In Bauer's video, the candidate shows he is not just good with young people, but that he has their support as well. Many of the people holding Bauer signs and attending rallies look to be college age or younger. In one scene, while Bauer is being interviewed by Chris Matthews on the CNBC show *Hardball*, a cadre of young people stands in the background holding signs. Matthews acknowledges Bauer's youth support when he leans over to Bauer and says, "Gary, I see you brought your troops with you." The crowd of young people cheers.

The videos of Forbes, McCain, and Bradley also show their candidate in a number of fatherly scenes. In addition to being seen with his own children, Forbes talks with African-American children and members of a high school band. He jokingly asks them if they are ready to play in his inaugural parade. McCain is shown playing with and reading to his kids. In Bradley's video, the candidate bends over to put his signature on a campaign sign held by a young girl. His act of bending down for the girl demonstrates that, although more than six-feet tall, the candidate is considerate enough to make himself accessible to all Americans.

The use of children in the primary videos is consistent with their use in presidential TV ad spots. Sherr (1999), in a qualitative analysis of about a thousand presidential general election commercials from 1952 to 1996, found that images of children are one of the key staples of ads. One of the benefits of including smiling children is to invoke "patriotic sentimentality and optimism that can be carried over to the sponsoring candidate" (p. 57).

The candidate as "hero" and "official keeper of American values" was presented in five of the six videos. The most notable use of the hero role came in McCain's video. In fact, the video's first lines come from a narrator who says: "At a time when America is searching for heroes to lead us, it has the genuine article in John McCain." The candidate is then shown in a leather jacket, talking with voters. McCain is shown as heroic during his service in Vietnam as well as his service in Congress. When the narrator discusses McCain's fight for campaign finance reform, the senator is shown working hard in his office.

As might be expected, the candidates are shown as the "official keeper" of many different "American values." Bauer's video is heavily weighted toward morality values, such as abortion. In one scene he is shown on *Meet the Press* defending his anti-abortion values: "In *Roe vs. Wade* the Supreme Court basically said that our children, our unborn children, can be treated like they were Styrofoam cups, that they had no rights under the Constitution. That's a national tragedy. America is better than one and a half million abortions a year and it would be a very big priority for me." Near the end of McCain's video, the candidate directly addresses the camera and talks about the values of freedom: "My campaign for president of the United States is built on one word: freedom. I'm running to advance human freedom at home and abroad and to ensure that all Americans have the freedom to live up to their highest hopes."

The videos of Bush, Bradley, and Forbes use outside sources, such as the media, to validate the candidates' high values. In Bush's video, a newspaper clip from *The Abilene Reporter-News* notes that the "governor calls for a new Texas culture of values, faith." During CNN coverage of Bradley's announcement speech, CNN notes that Bradley wants to fight against prejudice. Forbes's video uses testimonial quotes from civil rights activist Alveda King to authenticate Forbes's strong personal values.

The symbolic roles of "commander-in-chief," "chief budget setter," and "chief educator" are seen in four of the six primary videos. While Gore and McCain use their Vietnam experience to connect themselves to the armed forces, Bush's video presents the "commander-in-chief" role within the context of domestic law enforcement. Bush is seen at a youth boot camp, with an adult, black male in green military fatigues giving orders.

Just as was seen in his "official keeper of American values" role, Bush uses media validation to show he is the "chief budget setter" in his state of Texas. *Fortune* magazine notes that as governor, Bush has presided over a 15% jump in employment, a 47% decrease in the number of people on Texas' welfare rolls; and "at the same time, spending growth has fallen to its lowest rate in a quarter century." The videos of Bauer, Forbes, and McCain display the same symbolic role by talking about their tax plans.

The role of "chief educator" is used the most by Bush, who speaks about educational reform and also has the media validate his experience in this area. Bush promises educational excellence, saying, "It's a promise I will make and I hope you all make as well—is that we will have the best education system in the world. And that no child will get left behind." The screen then fades to a quote from *Business Week* magazine: "On a national level, the success of Bush's education initiatives is crucial to recasting the Republican Party in his 'Compassionate Conservative' image." In Gore's video, the vice president pledges to make "revolutionary" changes in education should he be elected president. Bauer and Forbes display this symbolic role by arguing favorably for school vouchers.

While the "world leader" role was exhibited in only one primary video, its use is worth noting because it is magazine publisher Forbes, not the vice president or the governor of Texas, who tries on this role for size. Forbes makes the most of his Reagan administration experience as the former chairman of the board that oversaw Radio Free Europe, which served as a means to communicate Western news to people behind the iron curtain during the time they were under Communist domination. Frank Shakespeare, former ambassador to Portugal and The Vatican, notes that Forbes "had to steep himself in the knowledge of these countries, the issues at play." Shakespeare adds that Forbes's success in this international role was even more important because "by coincidence, he did it at maybe the most sensitive time in history." Footage is then shown of the Berlin Wall coming down. This image insinuates that Forbes had a hand in the dismantling of communism in Eastern Europe. Later, Forbes is shown at an event talking with former President Reagan and former Soviet leader Mikhail Gorbachev. Forbes's video also notes that former Polish leader Lec Walesa "made a point of seeking Steve out" on a recent trip to America.

The presidential campaign films of Gore and Bush displayed roughly the same percentage of Roberts's presidential symbolic roles (75%) as did the six primary videos (70%). Just like the primary videos, the two films also presented the roles of "great communicator," "chief visionary," and "father figure." Bush talks about his vision while riding through his ranch in his jeep: "I think in order to be a good president, first and foremost you have to know where you want to lead. I want to lead America to a day that everybody in this country feels that the great American dream belongs to them as much as anybody else if they're willing to work for it." Bush also uses his jeep as the platform to talk about how he is the official keeper of American values: "This country's values are so strong and the concept of entrepreneurship, or family, or freedom, is such a powerful, powerful part of the American experience, that somebody who's newly arrived to this country, um, can be just as much an American as somebody who's been here for generations."

Gore's campaign film uses the "father figure" symbolic role more than the other roles. Photos of Gore campaigning with his children serve to blend this fatherly role with his government service. To add a softer touch, other photos show Gore reading to his daughters, and Gore's son, then a small child, pretending to shave with his dad. Tipper Gore adds that Gore always was there for his kids, even for the small things: "Family vacations were a very special time, and he enjoyed them as much as the kids did." Gore is then seen with his kids at Pawleys Island, South Carolina; on the Colorado River, in the Grand Canyon; and at Center Hill Lake, Tennessee.

One symbolic role presented in Gore's campaign film that is omitted from his primary video is that of "world leader." Toward the end of the campaign film, Gore is seen with South African president Nelson Mandela. For the most part, however, the primary videos and campaign films are equally rich in their use of symbolic roles to ritualistically display the candidates as presidential hopefuls who looks legitimately "presidential."

THE USE OF PEOPLE, LOCATIONS IN THE VIDEOS TO CREATE A REALISTIC CULTURAL MILIEU

With regard to documentary techniques, all of the presidential primary videos followed the tradition of focusing on real people and authentic events and locations, as opposed to using actors and sound stages. The types of people seen in the primary videos reflect the candidates' desire to be identified with a diverse group of potential voters [see Table 3]. All six primary videos include African Americans, children, senior citizens, white-collar workers, and women. Locations seen in a majority of the videos include rural settings (5 videos), unidentified offices (5 videos), political rallies (5 videos), and classrooms (4 videos) [see Table 4].

Members of the candidates' families are seen in five of the videos. Many candidates took this to the extreme, featuring testimonials from their wives, brothers, and daughters. On the other end of the spectrum, Bradley omits all references to his family, including any mention of his wife.

The Bush campaign is the only one to include footage of Hispanics; they are seen in both his primary video and campaign film. The heavy use of

Table 3.
Types of People Seen in the Primary Videos and Campaign Films

	Bill Bradley	Al Gore	Gary Bauer	George W. Bush	Steve Forbes	John McCain	Gore's campaign film	Bush's campaign film
Children	X	X	X	X	X	X	X	X
Senior citizens	X	X	X	X	X	X	X	X
Women	X	X	X	X	X	X	X	X
Asians		X				X	X	
African-Americans	X	X	X	X	X	X	X	X
Hispanics				X				X
Veterans		X					X	X
Disabled				X				
Blue-collar workers			X	X	X	X	X	X
White-collar workers	X	X	X	X	X	X	X	X
Members of candidates' family		X	X	X	X	X	X	X

Hispanics by Bush highlights the Texas governor's attempt to reach out to the fastest growing segment of the U.S. population (Loza, 1988). Hispanics are estimated to compose 20% of the population by 2010, making it the largest U.S. minority group (Lambro, 1999). The Hispanic outreach displayed in Bush's primary video also could be seen in his Internet, newspaper, and 30-second TV spot advertising during the primary campaign (Len-Rios, 2000; Nicholson, 1999). Research by Len-Rios found that Bush's "En Español" web site was particularly aggressive in wooing all types of Hispanics, differentiating his message among "distinct Hispanic populations" (p. 2). Bush's efforts were met by a receptive audience: A Battleground Poll conducted in January 2000 found that Hispanics preferred Bush to Gore by 51% to 38% (Cohen, 2000).

Table 4.
Types of Locations Seen in the Primary Videos and Campaign Films

	Bill Bradley	Al Gore	Gary Bauer	George W. Bush	Steve Forbes	John McCain	Gore's campaign film	Bush's campaign film
Office not identified		X	X	X	X	X	X	X
Oval Office		X	X					
Their official office			X			X	X	X
Military setting		X				X	X	X
Foreign country					X	X	X	X
Classroom			X	X	X	X	X	X
Industrial		X					X	X
Athletic	X			X			X	X
Their home		X			X	X	X	X
Rally	X		X	X	X	X	X	X
Urban			X		X		X	X
Rural		X	X	X	X	X	X	X
Inside or outside of Congress		X	X			X		

How the campaigns present different types of people can be grouped into two main themes: those with and without speaking roles. Bush's video typifies the seen-but-not-heard-from use of "real" people. Bush is seen reaching out to and connecting with a mix of Americans, including many African Americans and Hispanics. But no one speaks in Bush's video except the candidate. Forbes's video exemplifies the use of testimonials from "real" people. Forbes's video uses "man-on-the-street" type interviews from a wide cross-section of Americans—senior citizens, baby boomers, college students—to connect the wealthy magazine publisher with the average American. The technique is similar to what is seen in Ronald Reagan's 1984 campaign film, "A New Beginning," which includes a collage of testimonials from an ethnically diverse group of blue-collar and white-collar workers either outdoors or at their places of business, speaking favorably of President Reagan and his policies. In Forbes's primary video, as in Reagan's campaign film, the "man-on-the-street" technique creates a "reality" that shifts attention away from the fact that the video is political advertising manufactured by high-level campaign operatives.

The variety of locations seen in the videos also cleverly connects the candidates to many types of Americans. To help form a connection with some of the most important presidential primary voters, the candidates often are seen in Iowa and New Hampshire. Gore talks with voters in Bedford, New Hampshire. With a bright red tractor in the background, Bush speaks to a large midwestern crowd; Forbes is interviewed by a reporter in front of a grain silo in the Midwest.

Other locations help legitimate the candidate. Not surprisingly, Vice President Gore gets to look presidential in his video by including scenes of himself at the White House. On the other end of the spectrum, Gary Bauer, a man unknown to most Americans, displays multiple photos of himself inside the Oval Office during the Reagan administration to give stature and legitimacy to his presidential ambition. In fact, Bauer's video includes more scenes of the White House than any other video. Early in Bush's video, the candidate tries to look presidential as he is shown—in slow motion—taking the oath of office to become governor of Texas. To play up McCain's Washington experience and credentials, there are many shots of the Arizona senator on Capitol Hill and in his Senate office.

There were 11 types of people that were coded for in the content analysis. The six presidential primary videos displayed them a combined 67% of the time. There also were 13 types of locations that were coded for. The videos showed those locations 49% of the time. The two campaign films presented these people and locations more of the time, 77% and 85%, respectively.

Unlike the primary videos, the campaign films used popular culture and historical images to connect the candidates to the voters. Bush's campaign film exhibits this technique the most. Toward the end of the film, the candidate says in a speech, "Our great country was built by people who never gave up, and never gave in." Images shown during his remarks include footage of Willie Mays swinging at a pitch, Boy Scouts, the D-Day landing in Europe, General H. Norman Schwarzkopf giving a press briefing during Operation Desert Storm, and the flag raising after the battle of Iwo Jima. Short sound bites also are included from President Reagan's

Berlin Wall speech ("Mr. Gorbachev, tear down this wall"), President Kennedy's inaugural ("Ask not what your country can do for you"), Martin Luther King, Jr.'s Lincoln Memorial speech ("I have a dream today"), and President Richard Nixon's conversation with the Apollo astronauts ("Because of what you have done, the heavens have become a part of man's world").

CONCLUSIONS

Content analysis has revealed answers to some key questions about presidential primary videocassettes. First, the videos tend to have a balanced mix of image and issue appeals. This distinguishes them from the campaign films, which were only image-based. In trying to answer the question of what function the primary videos serve in presidential campaigning, these findings suggest that the videos serve a clear educational function to explain the candidates' stand on key public policy issues. This function seems quite different from that of the campaign films, which merely soften the candidates' personal image in the mind of viewers.

The issue orientation of the primary videos also is seen in how the videos displayed the many presidential symbolic roles, archetypal images, people, and locations that were coded for. One clear example of this difference is evident when comparing how Bush fit into the symbolic role of "chief educator." In his primary video, the Texas governor's educational record is spelled out and the candidate speaks in favor of educational testing standards. In his campaign film, however, Bush says vaguely that "reading is the new civil right."

Many candidates displayed a majority of the presidential symbolic roles and archetypal images as well as people and locations that were coded for [see Table 5]. The primary videos of Gore (80%), McCain (80%), and Bauer (70%) were notably high in the percentage of Morreale's archetypal images displayed. Roberts's presidential symbolic roles were tried on 80% of the time in the primary videos of Bush, Bauer, Forbes, and McCain. Gore and Bradley displayed those roles just 50% of the time.

Exploring presidential primary videos and campaign films helps illuminate research done on presidential imagery, performance, and campaign strategy. For example, some scholars, such as Misciagno, argue that the image of the presidency is in decline due to the erosion of the president's private sphere (1996, p. 329). Yet much of what is shown in these videos and films invites the viewer into a candidate's private life. This helps to break down the wall that separates a presidential candidate's public life from his personal life. This finding is consistent with the trend toward politicians creating a "public intimacy" between politicians and the voters (Jamieson, 1988, p. 182).

Table 5.
Total Percentages Displayed

	Bill Bradley	Al Gore	Gary Bauer	George W. Bush	Steve Forbes	John McCain	Gore's campaign film	Bush's campaign film
Morreale's archetypes	20%	80%	70%	40%	50%	80%	80%	80%
Roberts' symbolic roles	50%	50%	80%	80%	80%	80%	90%	60%
Different types of people seen	45%	64%	73%	82%	64%	73%	82%	82%
Different types of locations seen	15%	46%	69%	38%	54%	69%	85%	85%

In the 2000 race, the primary videos and campaign films pushed the boundaries of public intimacy. McCain's video details the personal torment McCain experienced as a prisoner of war, and McCain's wife invites viewers into their family life by recounting how they adopted a foreign child in desperate need of medical help. In the Gore campaign film, Tipper Gore talks openly about the "clinical depression" she suffered after their son was hit by a car. In George W. Bush's campaign film, mother Barbara Bush shares with viewers how her son helped her cope with the feelings of loss after the death of her daughter Robin.

This need for public intimacy may exist partly because as the voting public becomes less and less partisan (Oppenheimer, 1996; Cook, 1994), and campaigns become more and more candidate-centered (Troy, 1996), the successful campaigns are the ones that try to show their candidate as mirroring society (as being "one of us")—as opposed to winning points by making narrow political party appeals.

This use of public intimacy also aligns the films closely with the techniques of documentary film. As John Grierson, one of the founders of the documentary movement, wrote during its early days: "Documentary can achieve an intimacy of knowledge and effect impossible to the shim-sham mechanics of the studio, and the lily-fingered interpretations of the metropolitan actor" (Barsam, 1992).

One potentially "intimate" issue that most of the candidates tread lightly over is how to address the presidency of Bill Clinton. Not surprisingly, the videos of all four Republican challengers speak of the Clinton years in negative tones. However, only Bauer's video attacks Clinton by name; the videos of Bush, Forbes, and McCain opt for more oblique, unnamed slaps at Clinton.

Bush's primary video is representative of this subtle but strategic "negative ad" approach. Toward the end of the videos, Bush takes a swipe at President Clinton's moral character and says he will change things for the better. Bush says: "And I know this, that if I'm fortunate enough to become the president of the United States, when I put my hand on the Bible, I will swear to not only uphold the laws of the land, I will swear to uphold the dignity and the honor of the office to which I've been elected, so help me God." Bush raises his right hand as he says the last part of the sentence, symbolically taking the oath of office in front of the crowd. The crowd cheers. In this way, viewers are invited to compare the character of a "President George W. Bush" to the character of President Clinton.

In one brief segment of McCain's video, a combination of visual and verbal information achieves a subtle attack on Clinton. As the video's narrator says, "At a time when some leaders let us down," the visual shown over the remark is of the White House.

Only Bauer's video attacks President Clinton by name. Near the end of the video, Bauer directly addresses the camera. He says: "Today our nation is at a crossroads. Will we continue down our current path following the example set by Bill Clinton? Or will we, the great conservative majority, stand up once and for all and make our country the shining city on a hill that Ronald Reagan always dreamed it would be?"

Gore says nothing positive or negative about Bill Clinton in his video. Instead, Clinton is shown in an interview in the Oval Office talking about why he asked Gore to be his vice president. He says he picked Gore because "he knew a lot about things I didn't know much about."

The findings so far in the frame analysis and content analysis have provided many answers to questions dealing with how presidential primary videos function in a campaign. These answers have been revealed through the work of academically trained coders. While this exercise has been enlightening, the findings so far have been necessarily limited by the fact that the coders have no personal connection to the videos. The next step in further understanding the function of primary videos is to conduct in-depth interviews with the videos' producers. In other words, it is one thing to show what academically trained coders see through the lens of qualitiative and quanitative methods, but a more meaningful vision of the videos can be obtained by adding the perspective of the men and women who created them. The producers of the videos can confirm or clarify findings already presented. They also can lead the inquiry into these videos into new directions. In short, they can answer questions that have yet to be asked.

Chapter Five

From the Producer's Perspective: Interviews with Producers of the 2000 Campaign Videocassettes

Interviews with the producers of presidential primary videos adds a key element to answering the question of what function the videos serve in primary campaigning. In McCracken's (1988) book reviewing the literature and techniques of "the long interview," he argues: "The long interview gives us the opportunity to step into the mind of another person, to see and experience the world as they do themselves.... Every social scientific study is improved by a clearer understanding of the beliefs and experiences of the actors in question" (p. 9). Lindlof (1995) adds that interviews also can be used in "verifying, validating, or commenting on data obtained from other sources" (p. 166). For this reason, video producer interviews for this study were conducted after the frame analysis and content analysis methods were completed and analyzed.

In-depth interviews have been used frequently in communications research. Taylor, Hoy and Haley (1996) used interviews with advertising executives in France to expand depth and meaning to previous quantitative content analysis findings on French advertising practices. The research team conducted 11 in-depth interviews ranging from 45 minutes to more than two hours (p. 4). In addition, they used a five-question open-ended interview guide that provided for much interaction (p. 5). This strategy is consistent with McCracken's (1988) interviewing procedure, which also calls for "active listening," guarding against being too obtrusive, and asking broad "grand tour" questions early on to stimulate the initial conversation.

The interviews for this study lasted at least a half hour and were audiotaped with the permission of the participants, who signed a consent form.

The tapes were then transcribed verbatim. Their responses were analyzed for themes with regard to what function the videos played in the primary and what frames the producers thought they were using in their videos. The interview guide included questions designed to elicit insight into what function the videos had in the campaign:

Please tell me a little about your background in political campaign work. What other videos/TV spot ads have you done? For which candidates?

Tell me about your work, your title, your responsibilities for this campaign?

Whom did you report to in the campaign?

What were your instructions when you went about making the candidate's video?

How many people worked with you to make the video?

What function did the video play in your candidate's overall campaign strategy?

How much did the video cost to produce?

Tell me about these candidate videos as a method of disseminating political information. How many were made? Whom were the videos targeted to? What were the demographics of the target? Why?

What was the primary message that you were trying to get across to viewers? Why?

What verbal messages in the video did you want to stand out the most? Why?

What visuals in the video did you want to stand out the most? Why?

What effect did you want the video to have on viewers? Why?

Qualitative interviews with the producers of the presidential primary videocassettes of the 2000 election were designed to confirm and expand on findings previously made in the frame analysis and content analysis chapters. The in-depth interviews also provide an opportunity to get an insider's view of the function of videocassette campaigning.

The interviews were conducted by telephone during January and February 2001 with the producers of the videos for Gary Bauer (Tom Edmonds), John McCain (Paul Curcio), Steve Forbes (Paul Sanderson), and Al Gore (William Knapp). The producers for the videos of George W. Bush and Bill Bradley declined to be interviewed. The interviews ranged in time from 30 minutes to 45 minutes. The interviews were audiotaped and transcripts were made from each tape to explore various themes.

What emerged from the data are numerous common themes among the producers as to how and why the videocassettes were created. There are, too, many differences between the campaigns as to the function the videos—as well as the producers—played in the overall primary campaign strategy.

The first portion of this chapter separately reviews comments made by each producer. Their answers in this section help to fill out the description of each video's frame and, particularly, each video's image and issue information. Later in the chapter, the videos are explored as a combined unit in order to find key common themes. These common themes revolve around issues of: how the videos were used; how they were pretested; how the images and issues were selected; why the videos used media validation; why the videos used the frames they did; who the audience was; and how connected the producers were with the campaigns.

INTERVIEW WITH WILLIAM KNAPP, CO-PRODUCER OF AL GORE'S VIDEO

For years, Squire Knapp Dunn Communications, which is based in Washington, D.C., has been the leading Democratic advertising firm. Veteran political consultant Bob Squire, who died in January 2000 on the same day as the Iowa caucuses, produced advertising for countless members of Congress and senators, as well as for presidents ranging from Jimmy Carter to Bill Clinton. Squire directed and co-produced Gore's presidential primary videocassette. Next to Squire, William Knapp was most closely connected to the writing, interviewing, and production of "The Al Gore Story."

Knapp agreed that the "small-town values" frame was the dominant story line in Gore's video. He said there were several reasons the campaign chose to use that frame. With the videocassette's debut in early summer 1999, this was the first advertising to reach Iowa and New Hampshire voters. The videocassette was designed to set a positive tone before the inevitable flood of issue-based TV spots. Also, vice presidents traditionally have a hard time getting out from under the shadow of the president, and Gore's videocassette provided a vehicle for reintroducing Gore to the Democratic Party as well as the rest of the American people.

Finally, Knapp said Gore's video needed to show that his personal background was as interesting and compelling as that of his opponent in the Democratic primary, Bill Bradley. Bradley had been a Rhodes scholar, a professional basketball player, and a U.S. senator. Knapp said the message was clear that Gore had to match Bradley biography for biography:

We didn't want to cede that to [Bradley]. And we wanted to make it clear to people, you know, what values actually motivated Al Gore, beyond the stereotype. So we saw it as an important piece of inoculation. To get our story out before the caricature of us could be used against us. I mean there was a pre-existing caricature. You know, vice presidents are characterized in certain ways, it happens naturally. But we didn't want to give Bradley the chance to take that sort of loose, amorphous characterization and then solidify it against us in some way. We wanted to get in there and sort of redefine us, broaden the description of who we were. So it was important in that regard.

The use of humor in Gore's video also served the goal of changing the vice president's stereotype as something of a wooden soldier. According to Knapp, clips of Gore on *The Late Show with David Letterman* provided a good opportunity to do that. "One of these things is to share that this guy actually does have values and does care about things and there's actually blood in his veins, as opposed to the stereotype of what his was," he said.

The inclusion of Gore's Vietnam experience was a key element of the small-town values frame. Knapp said those segments of the video really affected the impression voters had of Gore. "I can't tell you how important that was for people to learn," he said. "They had no idea that he went. And it was totally the opposite of Clinton's experience." The video's unspoken comparison to Clinton's draft evasion during Vietnam furthered Gore's wish to be seen as his own man.

Knapp agreed that "The Al Gore Story" was primarily an image-based ad. He said the video avoided detailed policy appeals because the campaign felt this aspect of the campaign was already going strongly for Gore. "Let me tell you, we didn't have a problem with issues with this crowd," he said.

INTERVIEW WITH PAUL CURCIO, PRODUCER OF JOHN McCAIN'S VIDEO

Paul Curcio is a partner with Stevens Reed Curcio & Company, which is located in Alexandria, Virginia. The firm has done ads for Republican candidates such as Susan Collins, George Allen, and for Bob Dole and Kemp in 1996. They also did the famous "Tank" ad for George Bush's 1988 presidential campaign that attacked Democratic nominee Michael Dukakis by showing footage of him riding in a tank. Curcio, who started his career in the late 1970s at a New York ad agency handling accounts for Scope, Zest, and Pepto-Bismol, made his name politically during 10 years at the National Republican Senatorial Committee.

In 1998, Curcio wrote and produced advertising for Senator John McCain's successful re-election effort in Arizona. The tagline for McCain's 1998 Senate ads became the title for his 2000 presidential primary video: "The Character to Do What's Right, the Courage to Fight for It."

Curcio said his instructions in making McCain's primary videocassette were to try to tell McCain's life story in a way that connected the values he learned in his personal background to his political platform:

The assumption was—and I think the assumption was correct—the more that people knew about McCain, particularly about the Vietnam part of his life, the more credibility that he would have. So that if he stands up and says, "I pledge to you that I will stop this," "I will not do that," "This practice will end," ... you would have a tendency, people would have a tendency to believe McCain. Because if you knew what he had endured and never buckled, then surely if he wasn't afraid of ... Communists in North Vietnam, then why on earth would he be afraid of some political leader in Washington, D.C.?

The values frame of personal character and political courage translated best verbally with lines such as "putting America's interest ahead of his own," and "he's a man that we can believe and believe in," according to Curcio. In both cases, a connection is made between the personal and professional values of McCain. In the case of "putting America's interest ahead of his own," the personal risks of flying a jet during wartime are compared to the political risks of supporting controversial issues such as campaign finance reform. Curcio said connecting those thoughts would have been difficult for almost any candidate except McCain:

Writing for McCain, one of the things I found that was very interesting and in some ways sounds corny, I suppose, is that it was uplifting, is that you have access and almost the permission to use language and sentiments that you couldn't use for most other politicians....It would sound like, "Come on, don't sound this pompous." But for McCain, and I don't remember all the language in there but, you know, "a man you can believe and believe in," "more tested and better prepared," "the character to do what's right and the courage to fight for it." I mean, that's stuff that's pushing the limits for somebody else. But you can say those for McCain and have no problem. So it's kind of nice to write for someone like that and, again, it's kind of a once-in-a-lifetime thing because you'll never have some one like that again. So all the stable of words and sentiments, you know, use them once and that's it.

Curcio said the inclusion of both image and issue appeals in McCain's video reflected the need of the campaign to tell the senator's very personal story while at the same time reach out to primary voters, who expect talk about the issues.

INTERVIEW WITH TOM EDMONDS, PRODUCER OF GARY BAUER'S VIDEO

Tom Edmonds, who is president of the Washington, D.C.-based Edmonds Associates, has spent more than 20 years in the political media business. It is no surprise that Bauer, who was one of the most conservative candidates for the Republican nomination, chose Edmonds. In the early 1980s, Edmonds consulted for the National Conservative Political Action Committee. In 1994, Edmonds, who produced media for the National Rifle Association's 1994 election effort, was credited as being a key player in the Republican takeover of Congress. It is also no surprise that Edmonds was able to re-create the Reagan presidency so seamlessly in Bauer's video. Several years ago the Republican National Committee selected Edmonds to produce the official documentary of the Reagan presidency, titled "Ronald Reagan: An American President."

The in-depth interview with Edmonds confirmed the main findings from the frame analysis and content analysis chapters. Frame analysis revealed that the dominant story line for Bauer's 19-minute video, titled "Who I Am and What I Believe," was that Bauer would "reclaim Reagan's legacy." Edmonds agreed that the videocassette, along with Bauer's other advertising, was designed to, as he said, "position himself as the heir apparent to Reagan ... to be where the Reaganites should go. You can look at the whole field of candidates and he saw this as a void." Edmonds said he accomplished this effect by tracking down "whatever pictures we could of Gary with Reagan, which were few and far between," and by wrapping "some of the trappings of Reagan around him."

Edmonds added that tying Bauer to Reagan served a key function other than attracting voters who are favorable to Reagan's conservative philosophy. Bauer's jobs during the Reagan administration demonstrated his connection to high-level federal government service. By showing Bauer with Reagan in the Oval Office, Edmonds said he was able to help his candidate look more presidential.

The video's heavy issue-orientation also served the function of legitimizing Bauer and broadening his appeal. Edmonds said that before his presidential run, Bauer was known almost solely as an anti-abortion advocate. Bauer's videocassette was designed to change that. In the video, Bauer addresses issues ranging from tax reform to school vouchers to a space-based, anti-missile defense shield. Edmonds said the issue orientation of the video was done because "if you did a poll and you said, 'Gary Bauer,' they would say, 'Right to Life.' ... You cannot get elected on just that one issue. I didn't want to run away from it. He wouldn't run away from it. But I did all those issues—there's just a litany of issues—and it was actually based on polling data. I'm not saying he does his life that way. But we definitely had a checklist of issues, and I wanted him to speak to each and every one of these issues."

INTERVIEW WITH PAUL SANDERSON, PRODUCER OF STEVE FORBES'S VIDEO

Paul Sanderson, a documentary filmmaker who also does corporate videos, had no political campaign advertising experience before agreeing to make Steve Forbes's 1996 presidential primary video. His Bernardsville, New Jersy, firm, Our Town Films, Inc., was tapped for the project because Sanderson had known and worked with the Forbes family for many years. Sanderson ended up gaining a lot of political communication experience in 1996: He produced and directed more than 100 TV ads and about 45 radio ads for Forbes. By the time Forbes decided to run in the 2000 race, Sanderson was the logical choice to do a new primary campaign videocassette, titled "A Rebirth of Freedom."

The values frame of "family values" and fighting for "individual freedom" was divided between the biographical and issue segments in the video because of instructions Sanderson received from the campaign. "The basic sense of it was...give them basic information, background on who the candidate is and what he stands for," he said.

One notable aspect of Forbes's video is how he is displayed in so many presidential symbolic roles, including being the only candidate to be seen in the "world leader" role. Mikhail Gorbachev, Lec Walesa, and Margaret Thatcher, the former leaders of the Soviet Union, Poland, and England, respectively, make appearances with Forbes in his video. Sanderson said the campaign saw the need to show voters that Forbes could fit into many presidential roles:

The first thing I did was talk to the pollster and he talked to me and we said, you know, "What do you need here?" ... The biggest issue probably in the whole thing was, "Was Steve presidential?" If people compared him in just terms of brains, I mean Steve would win hands down. But that's not what people vote totally on. Being presidential is the number one thing, and it was the number one thing against him. He didn't have a presidential look. He didn't look good. And he didn't present himself as far as the way he spoke and presented himself that way as presidential, which was something we needed to overcome.

Opening Forbes's 2000 videocassette with footage of his 1996 win in Arizona was another way of building up legitimacy by showing that the magazine publisher could attract voters in major states. Sanderson said Forbes looked transformed at that moment: "He was very good in his speech, very excited, more animated than he normally is....So he looked more presidential, felt more presidential."

Sanderson said Forbes's video was balanced between image and issue appeals because that was the format that made the most sense early in the primary campaign:

You take the point of view that someone who's watching it doesn't know anything about the candidate....And so the first thing they need to know is, "Why is he running for president?" and "Why should he be president?" I mean, "What credentials does he have?" You know, "Who the hell is he?" And then, all right, now I know who he is, "What does he think, what does he want to do?" So I mean that's pretty basic, in my opinion. That's the way I would want to do it.

COMMON THEMES AMONG THE PRODUCERS OF THE VIDEOS

The major themes that run through the interviews with the producers help answer the main research question "What function do presidential primary videos serve in a primary campaign?" As a rule, the videocassettes were used as a fund-raiser, a surrogate speaker, and an inoculator.

The candidates sent the videos out early in the campaign season to establish an initial image. The videos tended to be pretested in some way before they were widely distributed. The images and issues in the video were predetermined based on extensive polling data from the campaign. All the producers used media validation because they felt it gave their candidate and their candidate's video increased credibility and legitimacy. Finally, all the producers saw distinct strategic advantages in using candidate videocassettes.

Fund-Raiser, Surrogate Speaker, Inoculator

Many of the videos were designed specifically to be fund-raising vehicles. Bauer's video, which typifies this approach, employed what the campaign termed a "friend-to-friend" program whereby those who received the video were asked to do two things: contribute financially to the campaign and show the video to 10 of their friends and family. They, in turn, were asked to give money and show the video to 10 of their friends. Edmonds says the fund-raising arm of Bauer's campaign monitored the progress of this effort.

McCain's video similarly included a segment where the candidate called on viewers to financially donate to his candidacy. Curcio said the main effect of this was clear: "It was an attempt after people saw all this you wanted them to be politically motivated to say, 'This is a guy we can really be proud of as our president,' and then get them to contribute to the campaign."

Forbes's video, which included no financial call to action, was nonetheless debuted in front of 1,500 contributors at a fund-raiser at the Waldorf Astoria Hotel in New York in the summer of 1999. Knapp said Gore's video was not used much as a fund-raising instrument.

All the producers agreed that their videos served well as a surrogate speaker at events and gatherings where the candidate could not attend. These gathering were either too small to warrant a visit by the candidate or the candidate was committed to be elsewhere. Knapp said Gore supporters also would use his video in more personal ways to attract voters: "Part of this was an organizing tool for, you know, if people would have coffee klatches and Gore couldn't make it, they could show it, you know. This was used a little bit sort of in the grass roots in that way as well. It wasn't all just about mailing it."

In the case of Forbes, the video also was used as sort of an introductory speaker to warm up crowds at events in Iowa that were being visited by the candidate's campaign bus. "They used it on the bus tour. They showed it every time they stopped," Sanderson said. Knapp said candidate videos also are good tools to inoculate voters who might have pre-existing misperceptions about the candidate.

Pretesting the videos.   The videocassettes were pretested prior to mass distribution to make sure that the messages—and the messengers—were effectively persuading voters. Many of the campaigns ran focus groups to test voter response to what they saw in the videos. Sanderson said he was mostly pleased with focus group reactions to his video: "We would show [Forbes's video] in the focus groups and you wouldn't believe the difference it made.... They said, 'Oh, I didn't know that. I didn't realize he did that.' You kind of wish that the same one filmmaker would make a video on all the candidates and then we'd have a fair way of judging them and really get to know them."

While much of the feedback from the focus groups was positive, negative responses also helped the campaigns improve the videos. Sanderson said focus group participants, who were armed with electronic meters that could be manipulated to go up or down to denote positive or negative reaction to what was being viewed, collectively noted their displeasure with Tim Forbes, who gave several testimonials in Steve Forbes's video: "I don't think Tim's a particularly bad-looking person, but it was something about him that irritated people that we never would have perceived. So we limited him on camera a little bit."

While Gore's video was not reviewed by focus groups, Knapp said the video did receive some pretesting: "We sent it to the Iowa coordinator. We sent it to people in our campaign in Iowa, for example, who knew the caucus goers inside and out. And they thought it would be effective. And it wasn't that expensive to send, and we knew it would do no harm. In other words, it was an important piece of the tactical game we wanted to play. It served our broader strategy. So we didn't see a need to pay for testing with focus groups."

What images and issues made it into the videos were often selected based on extensive polling data from the campaign. Knapp said Gore's pollster at the time had a lot of input on the video. "The messages and key strategic themes in it were heavily poll tested," Knapp said. Sanderson said the Forbes campaign also relied on polls when it came to making "A Rebirth of Freedom":

Basically, the whole video was based on using information from the pollsters. In other words, what people either like, dislike or want to know about Steve Forbes. ...The very first things that were done were the polls and finding out how...Steve stacks up to how people think of him. So, I mean, it just makes a lot of sense. The polls tell you what people are thinking, and usually polls are pretty accurate. At least I was shocked at how accurate they were when I first got into it.

Bauer's campaign included information from polls in its decision-making process of finding an overall unique selling proposition for the candidate: "We had looked at primary polling and secondary polling and what the positions of the other candidates were and where the areas of opportunity were. So it was a collaborative effort," Edmonds said.

McCain's campaign also used polling data to aid in issue selection for the video. Curcio said that mentioning McCain's support of Internet filtering technology was "a way to talk to social conservatives." However, Curcio also said that the video's inclusion of certain economic issues, such as the marriage penalty tax and the inheritance tax, did not need to be justified by poll results. "Intuitively, you just know in a Republican primary you talk about taxes," he said.

Setting a positive tone. All the videos were sent out early in the campaign season to establish an initial, positive image. Bauer's campaign began sending videos out in March 1999, mailing them in waves. The other campaigns distributed their videos in the late spring and early summer of 1999. Setting a positive tone was a key function of the videos. Knapp said this was especially true for Gore's video. "I wanted them to feel better about the guy. Like this is a decent, good guy who shares my values," he said. So the candidates did not attack each other in their videos. Even when the Republican candidates attacked Clinton, they did so subtly to preserve their positive tone. Curcio said this was the reason McCain's video never addressed Clinton by name, but still was able to score points with GOP voters:

We wanted this to be much more focused on the positive side of McCain than to start haranguing about Clinton. The other thing was you don't really need to say too much, certainly not to Republicans, about Clinton. All you need to do is show the White House and say, "At a time that some leaders let us down," you know? "Guess who we're talking about?" You can be very subtle. Keep the tone positive while still making the statement. What we were trying to do was say that this guy is the un-Clinton. Where Clinton is a coward, he is a hero, where Clinton is a liar, he tells you the truth. He's everything that Bill and Hillary Clinton aren't.

Media validation. All the producers used media validation because they felt it gave their candidate and their candidate's video increased credibility and legitimacy. Knapp said using testimonials from journalists such as John Seigenthaler of *The Nashville Tennessean* in his video also added to the positive tone he was trying to create:

I think most critically, it addresses a little bit of voter skepticism....It makes the video itself seem more accurate. It reassures them that what they're hearing is true. And in the case of journalism, as much as journalism writ large is taking it on the neck, there is a sense that, you know, there's a little bit of they're seekers of the truth. They tell the truth. They don't have a political ax to grind. And, you know, that's very useful as well. You get a little of the positive archetype of ... reporting and journalism.... There's a lot of negative baggage nowadays as well. But as part of a historical bio, you don't really pick up the negatives.

Sanderson said clips from broadcast and print media in Forbes's video replaced the need to have a narrator, which is typically included in political advertising to add a voice of authority:

Any time you hear a narrator, or you have someone who represents Steve Forbes saying how great Steve Forbes is, the first thing you do is say, "Well, of course you think Steve Forbes is great. He's paying you to say that." So you have to look for other validations from people that people know. And if being on the cover of *Time* magazine means that *Time* magazine thinks you're important enough to the American people to put you on the cover, that means you must be important enough to the American people. And that would be important to you as a potential voter. So it's pretty straightforward that having the media take you seriously means you're a serious candidate and that you're somebody who should be considered strongly.

Bauer's video, which included a narrator, used media validation to create a buzz among Republican voters who may not have known much about the conservative activist, according to Edmonds:

He is very good on his feet in unscripted situations. But also, I couldn't replicate some of these things. But also this did provide legitimacy to him. Which, you know, despite all of that exposure that he had had, his name ID was very, very small. So that was a way that communicated on two fronts simultaneously. You heard whatever it was he was saying, but in the context of being on *Meet the Press*, then he must be somebody....I wanted to show that he was a national person, you know, already had credentials. I wanted people to feel like they were the only ones who really didn't know this guy. "Gee, I must have missed something," you know? "Maybe it's me."

This heavy, bipartisan use of media validation belies the tough rhetoric presidential candidates sometime use against the press. Sanderson said that kind of inconsistency doesn't prevent video producers from including positive media references: "It is hypocritical. Of course it is. The thing about it is it's a game that people play, I guess. The thing is that the American people listen to the media."

Advantages of candidate videocassettes.   Finally, the producers agreed that presidential primary videocassettes exist because this type of advertising boasts several substantial advantages over 30-second TV spots. Sanderson, who did both Forbes's TV spot ads and video, said videocassettes are not bound by the limitations of TV ads:

The one thing that is sad about the 30-second spots is that it's so limited in what you can do. I mean [Forbes' campaign] used to give me scripts for those. And there would be three or four things that they wanted to say, and I'd say, "Listen. Nobody's going to remember all this." You got to really concentrate on one thing and do it well if you're going to have them remember anything in a 30-second spot. But in a longer format video, you have time to allow the viewer to kind of begin to for-mulate, you know, a sense of who the candidate is. If it's done right.

Curcio said the extensive biographical segment in primary videos is es-pecially effective because he believes a person's vote for president is an ex-tremely personal vote, more so than for other federal offices: "A campaign is helped to the degree that people know what kind of a person you are and basically like you. I think that's an important component in deciding who you are going to vote for. And so these things give you the luxury of 10 minutes to go into a lot of detail. You get a real window into someone's soul and what they're all about. I think that's important. The second ad-vantage is that, you know, you can target it quite well."

Knapp said some of the strengths of candidate videocassettes can also be weaknesses:

It requires an active—this is a positive but also a negative—it requires an active role from the person receiving it to take it out of the box, look at it, decide they're interested enough, put it in, and actually hit play. And in doing that you get them vested a little bit even before they see it. And I think there's a utility in that. You know, they say if someone gives you a dollar they'll definitely vote for you no matter what. In other words, if someone takes the time to do that and watch the thing from beginning to end, just by doing that and devoting some time to that, they'll remember you more, they'll know you more, they'll think you touched them more, that you care about them more, you know? So that helps. The disadvantage is that it requires someone to open up a box, look at the tape, and decide to look at it.

While Curcio and Knapp argue that the efficacy of videocassettes comes mainly during the early part of the primary campaign season, Sanderson said candidate videos can influence regular voters even up to election day: "The week before the vote, people are willing to watch half hours, or two weeks before the vote, when it's getting very intense in Iowa and New Hampshire. They're willing to watch something to help make their decision. They'll watch it if it's given to them or if it's on tele-vision—if they're really going to vote. So it can be an extremely power-ful thing."

DIFFERENCES AMONG THE VIDEOS

Even with all the similarities, each campaign used its candidate video-cassette in a slightly different way. The audience for the videos differed from campaign to campaign; The cost of the videos ranged considerably. And the connection and closeness the producers had with their cam-paigns were quite different. Finally, there is disagreement among the pro-ducers as to the future utility of candidate videocassettes.

Video Targeting

The audience for the videos, which ranged in price from $21,000 for Bauer's to around $100,000 for Forbes's, differed from campaign to campaign. Gore sent out about 10,000 videos to select groups in Iowa and New Hampshire: "These videos were targeted very much to strong Democrats, caucus-goers, and elite decision-makers in the Democratic process.... In Iowa, it was more caucus-goers. In New Hampshire, it was more, it was kind of the political chattering class" Knapp said. McCain, who did not contest Iowa, targeted his 50,000 videos in other states, such as New Hampshire and South Carolina. The campaign also made a special effort to mail the video to veterans in key states.

One constituency in particular—journalists—was courted by some candidates but shunned by others. Forbes's campaign in particular went out of its way to mail copies of the video to the media. Sanderson said journalists often would request the videos and use parts of it in their stories:

They depended on it for information....They probably asked for it more than we'd even give it to them. They all wanted B-roll of Steve. They all wanted to know some information about him. So they ate it up. Whether it affected them, I can't tell you. But as far as having information, the media can't get enough. And so they all know that these things are puff pieces in a certain sense. But that's why I say we tried very hard to keep it seeming not as puffy by not using a narrator, by using real people. But, yeah, the media used those all the time.

On the other end of the spectrum, Knapp said Gore's campaign did not want the media to see, and therefore report about, their video. "They put everything through their filter. We wanted real people to see this. We didn't want the press to interpret it," Knapp said. Nonetheless, journalists such as Connolly (1999) of *The Washington Post* obtained their own copies and wrote stories about the video that challenged the video's dominant frame that Gore came from small-town America. Knapp cited Connolly's article as one example of the kind of "ugly little spin," as he put it, that the Gore campaign wished to avoid.

Links Between the Campaigns and the Producers

The connection and closeness the producers had with their campaigns varied widely. Knapp was assisted by Gore himself in the production of his video, which is unusual for candidate videos as well as for TV spot ads. According to Knapp, "Basically our only direct report for this video was with Gore himself.... We talked to a lot of people in Tennessee. So we leaned a lot on him about who we should interview. And he had some strong opinions about who we should interview and who we shouldn't, and what stories were real and what stories were apocryphal."

Edmonds had previous dealings with Bauer and doing his presidential video was just one part of Bauer's advertising that he handled: "I did this because I had worked with Bauer before and I wanted to do his presidential campaign. . . . I wanted to do the media for his campaign, and indeed we did do that. So it was kind of a loss leader."

Some candidates used footage from their video in other advertising. This strategy helped to form a consistent theme for the campaign. But other candidates treated their video—and their producers—as a separate entity. Like Edmonds, Knapp's firm also produced both his candidate's TV spot ads and video. Because the video was one of the first pieces of advertising produced for Gore's presidential effort, the material gathered was available to be used by the candidate later in the campaign. "Some of the footage we got ended up being useful for ads later down the line. You know, it became part of our library which we could pull from," Knapp said. McCain's video was perhaps the most connected to the campaign's overall advertising effort. In addition to the video being sold on McCain's web site, text and images from the video were included on parts of the site.

Sanderson's role in Forbes's advertising was more comprehensive in 1996 than in 2000. In 1996 he was the main producer for both the video and the traditional TV and radio spots. This unified approach ended early in the 2000 race when Forbes brought in a separate TV spot producer: "They basically let me do my own thing. So I would go on the road and shoot Steve, but it was done as a separate thing from the ads, which was really a mistake. . . . All the footage that I was creating, I could have created lots of neat ads of what Steve was doing in the field. But that didn't happen." One exception to Sanderson's experience was in Iowa, where the campaign had him make special versions of the videos. Sanderson was asked to make an 8-minute version of Forbes's video as well as a 15-minute version that could be looped and played on cable television. Forbes's video also included a brief segment at the end explaining the rules of how to vote in Iowa's caucus.

The frame of reference the producers had when creating their video also varied. Some producers, such as Sanderson, had seen past presidential primary videos, while others, such as Knapp, looked at past presidential campaign films as their guide to what the video should look like.

The Future of Candidate Videos

Finally, the producers disagree somewhat as to the future utility of presidential primary videocassettes. Edmonds sees the videos' future as "clouded because of changes in technology." But Curcio is optimistic that this type of targeted, long-format advertising is here to stay, though with some changes:

I don't think they'll die off. I think the method of dissemination will become different. I don't think they'll die off because, you know, this society can change in a whole lot of ways—technologically, and sociologically, and demographically, and so forth—but I still believe when it's all said and done, that vote is a very personal vote. And these things provide … a very good tool to accomplish this early in a campaign, and I want to stress early. The method of dissemination probably will begin to evolve, and I think … much more of this will be done online.

CONCLUSIONS

It is clear from talking with the producers of the candidate videos for the 2000 presidential race that candidate videos serve several key, common functions in a political campaign. Political videocassettes are fundraisers, surrogate speakers, and inoculators. The videos, which are sculpted and fashioned by polling data and focus groups, are sent out early in the campaign to establish an initial, positive image. The dominant frames woven into the issue and image information of the videos help to further that positive tone as well as enhance the candidate in areas where he or she may be lacking.

But while the videos share some common functions, each campaigns targeted their videos to a slightly different audience based on the overall strategy of the campaign. The difference between how the campaigns dealt with media requests for candidate videos is especially noteworthy. Future research needs to investigate media interaction with presidential primary videocassettes.

Chapter 6

Conclusions

This study sought to demystify a type of political communication that Mundy (1995) called "a hot secret among political consultants": presidential primary campaign videocassettes. A variety of methods were used to explore the primary videocassettes of the Democratic and Republican presidential candidates—Gary Bauer, Bill Bradley, George W. Bush, Steve Forbes, Al Gore, and John McCain—who released presidential primary "meet the candidate videos" during the 2000 presidential primary.

The multiple method approach, which included frame analysis, quantitative content analysis, and in-depth interviews with the producers of these videos, was employed to provide answers to the study's main research questions.

By now it is clear that presidential primary campaign videocassettes serve a variety of key functions in a presidential race:

- The videocassettes are used as fund-raisers, surrogate speakers, and inoculators. Many candidates included segments in their videos in which they addressed the camera and asked viewers for donations. Most candidate videos provided contact information to be used in writing checks to the campaign. All the campaigns considered primary videos a key introductory speaker for their candidate early in the campaign, just as the candidates were emerging onto the public stage. Finally, several videocassette producers—especially those for Gore and Bauer—noted that their video was designed to inoculate their candidate against previous stereotypes that voters had about their candidate. The videocassettes were thus designed to change as well as create perceptions of the candidate.

- The videos, which include images and issues often based on polling data and focus groups, are sent out early in the campaign to establish an initial, positive image.

- The dominant frames woven into the issue and image information of the videos helped to further the positive tone as well as enhance the candidate in areas where the campaign felt he needed it. For the candidates of 2000, the frames were Bradley (leadership and electability); Gore (values); Bauer (reclaim Reagan's legacy); Bush (change); Forbes (values and individual freedom); and McCain (values). The values frame, seen in the videos of Gore, McCain, and Forbes, mostly is used to highlight the candidates'strong family ties. The values frame also is employed to connect the candidates' personal values to their policy agendas. Bauer's frame was used partly to add stature to the candidate, and Bush's frame helped set the tone for his "compassionate conservative" message. The video frames fit into the overall function that candidate videocassettes play in presidential primaries in that the frames allowed the campaigns to efficiently package up to 19 minutes of complex image and issue information into one or two dominant story lines. Packaging the information in this way aided the campaigns' efforts to influence voter perceptions early in the primary season.

- In addition, one other frame reached across party lines and was found in all six videos: mass media as supplier of validation, or, "I am qualified to be president because the media say I am." This frame helped establish legitimacy and credibility for the candidates' videos and for the candidates themselves. Bush's video uses multiple quotes from national and state publications to substantiate his record in Texas on taxes, welfare reform, and education. In Gore's video, the candidate's previous career as a journalist is compared favorably to the role of the politician: Both jobs are a form of noble public service. In the videos of Bradley, Bauer, Forbes, and McCain, these lesser known candidates are able to show themselves as nationally known and well-respected figures. While many political leaders like to tell voters that they shouldn't trust the media, the message in these direct-mail videos is that viewers should trust what they hear in the media. Also of note is that several candidates made their video available to the media in order to shape their coverage. Future research needs to investigate media interaction with presidential primary videocassettes. One question that needs to be addressed is how influential the videos are in shaping journalists' images of presidential candidates as they emerge onto the public stage.

- The heavy inclusion of presidential symbolic roles in most of the primary videos further adds to the videos' function as a tool to enhance the candidates' legitimacy in areas where the campaign felt it was needed. All the symbolic roles were displayed by at least some of the candidates. Of the 10 roles—"great communicator;" "chief visionary;" "hero;" "father figure;" "chief budget setter;" "official keeper of American values;" "commander-in-chief;" "chief legislator;" "world leader;" and "chief educator"—a few stand out. The most commonly used symbolic roles in the presidential primary videos were "great communicator," "chief visionary," and "father figure." All the primary videos modeled these three roles for fit and acceptability before the American public. The candidates usually displayed the communicator role by giving a speech in which they talk about key issues of the day. The visionary role, too, allowed the candidate to discuss important issues. The role of father figure served the function of softening the candidates' images and making them look like they shared the same family values as most voters. Other symbolic roles were used to alter existing perceptions of the candidate. The use of the "world leader" role by Forbes helped fill out the resume of the magazine publisher and aided in making him look more presidential. The exclusion of the world leader role in all other primary videos suggests that foreign policy concerns were not considered paramount during the 2000 presidential primary.

- The primary videos tend to have a balanced mix of image and issue appeals. The primary videos of Gary Bauer and Bill Bradley were classified as "primarily issue-based," while the videos of George W. Bush, John McCain, and Steve Forbes were classified as "truly balanced between image and issue appeals." Only Al Gore's video was classified as "primarily image-based." In trying to answer the question of what function the primary videos serve in presidential campaigning, one comes to the conclusion that the videos serve a clear educational function to explain the candidates' stands on key public policy issues. One of the key findings of this study is that while past political communication research has found the 30-second TV ad spots of politicians to be wanting in terms of issues and substance, presidential primary videos stand out as issue-rich (Joslyn, 1986; Just, Crigler and Wallach, 1990). Political advertising that is issue-based tends to produce greater voting intent and more positive attitudes about the candidate being promoted in the ad than do image-based ads (Kaid and Sanders, 1978; Thorson, Christ, and Caywood, 1991). The issue orientation of the primary videos often is reflected in how the videos displayed the many presidential symbolic roles, archetypal images, people, and locations that were coded for. Bush and Gore used the "chief educator" role to address education policy. Forbes used "man on the street" interviews with a diverse group of citizens to validate the candidate on issues such as the flat tax.

- But while the videos share some common functions, each campaign targeted its video to a slightly different audience based on the overall strategy of the campaign. Some candidates, such as McCain, targeted their videos to independents as well as the party faithful. On the other end of the spectrum, Gore's video was distributed mostly to Democratic activists. Also, the connection the producers had with their campaign varied widely. Some candidates used footage from their video in their other advertising. This strategy helped to form a consistent theme for the campaign. But other candidates treated their video—and their producers—as a separate entity. While the producer of Gore's video received advice from the candidate himself, Forbes's producer received little feedback from his candidate's campaign staff. Finally, there were differences between how the campaigns dealt with media requests for candidate videos. Some campaigns actively sought to use the videos to influence media coverage, while other campaigns made efforts to keep their videos out of the hands of the press. Regardless, most videos were obtained by journalists, who wrote both positive and negative stories about the information they found in the videos (Barker, 1999; Carney, 1999; Connolly, 1999; Kranish, 1999).

- The candidate videocassettes of 2000 bear a striking resemblance to those from decades past in terms of style and substance. Historically, candidate videos include a substantial mix of image and issue appeals, with biographical information being followed by the candidate talking about key issues of the day. While the videos were mostly positive, jabs at the opposition party were sometimes made, though intra-party attacks were almost unheard of. Most videocassettes were mailed to regular voters in Iowa and New Hampshire, while many candidates also targeted the videos to party activists in other states. Because the videos tended to be sent out early in the campaign season, the videos helped the candidates test the political waters, convincing some to continue and forcing some to drop out. Over the past 20 years changes in the technological, cultural, and political environments fueled the emergence and growth of candidate videocassette advertising.

- Lastly, presidential primary videos serve a different function from that of presidential campaign films. These films, which Morreale explored so thoroughly, are broadcast to a national TV audience during the Democratic and Republican national conventions. But presidential primary campaign direct mail videocassettes are targeted—or narrowcast—to party faithful during the early months of the primary campaign season. These different audiences and methods of dissemination help explain why presidential campaign films focus almost entirely on promoting pleasant images of the presidential nominee while the primary campaign videos concentrate far more on specific issues of the day to move potential voters to the polls. However, primary videos do visually share some of the key archetypes that Morreale found with regard to campaign films. The archetypes—that of the candidate as learning values from parents, having a hard-scrabble beginning in life, having a "love story" relationship with their spouse; being good with their children, coming from "small-town America," being athletic, being a modern Cincinnatus, displaying wartime heroism, associating with political party heroes, and having the power to restore the "American dream"—are seen in some of the videos. More than two-thirds of the primary videos displayed the candidate as learning values from parents, being good with their children, being athletic, having duty to their country, associating themselves with past party leaders, and having the power to restore the "American dream."

This study, which explores a unique, alternative type of primary campaign communication, expands political communication research done on other primary campaign and general election advertising activities. While Pfau et al. (1995) found that TV spot ads can exercise influence on voters' perception of candidates during primary campaigning, this study found that primary campaign videos also can alter voter perceptions. Sometimes the campaigns intentionally create these perception alterations in the form of the frames used in the primary videos. As the Gore video's producer, William Knapp, said during his in-depth interview, the "small-town values" frame was selected based on polling data that indicated that Gore needed to change his stereotype as a valueless creature of the Capitol.

The media validation included in the primary videos also was meant to alter voter perceptions. The clearest proof of this came in the comments of Tom Edmonds and Paul Sanderson, the producers for Gary Bauer and Steve Forbes, respectively. They said they hoped voters who saw the videocassettes' footage of their candidates on nationally broadcast public affairs shows such as *Meet the Press* would begin to think of their candidate as presidential.

Other political communication scholarship also dovetails with findings from this study. Devlin (1994) found that presidential candidates who advertised early and retain a fixed image fare well in comparison with candidates who produce multiple images. As was discussed in the in-depth interview, several campaigns made an effort to use footage from the primary video in other advertising. This technique not only saves time and money, it also aided the ability of the campaign to present a fixed image in the mind of voters.

This study shows not only the links research on candidate videos have with scholarship on other forms of political advertising, but areas of opportunity for further research in political communication. Researching presidential primary campaign communication—including primary videos—is significant because today it is primaries, not the traditional national nominating conventions, that select a presidential nominee. In today's primary-dominated nominating contests, the winners often get decided very early in the primary season based on a sense of "momentum" and "inevitability" that the winning candidates create. Future research needs to take presidential primary videos into account as one of the key tools candidates use to create that sense of momentum.

Another area of political communication research argues that presidential candidates cannot rely on the media to carry their message to primary voters. Media coverage by TV network newscasts during primaries has been shown to focus more on the "horse race" aspect of campaigning and less on explaining the specific issues the candidates are talking about (Speckman, 1999; Bartels, 1988). In addition, the "newshole" that journalists need to fill for each publication or broadcast tends to get smaller and smaller for presidential primary campaign news as the primary season progresses (Robinson and Sheehan, 1983). This trend is especially perilous for candidates because, as Roberts (1979, 1981) found, the impressions voters have about candidates form quite early during a campaign, and these impressions are aided by information disseminated through the media. Findings from the historical and in-depth interview chapters show that presidential candidates often try to use their candidate videocassettes to alter media perceptions—and coverage—of their candidate. Future research needs to examine how effective primary videocassettes are at influencing how journalists cover presidential candidates.

Another key question that future research can address is how effective these candidate videos are at creating or changing candidate perceptions among voters in key primary and caucus states such as Iowa, New Hampshire, and South Carolina. Do viewers of these videos focus on the same frames found in this study, or do they intertwine candidate video frames with their individual and cultural frames to construct a separate meaning?

In any event, this study is useful in that it built on existing general knowledge of presidential advertising, primary campaign strategies, and direct marketing techniques. Further, it is hoped that the present study may contribute to political communication research by adding knowledge about what function presidential primary videos play in presidential primary campaigns. Primary videos, their messages, and their functions are fruitful areas for political communication scholarship. As technology changes from videocassettes to the next generation of innovation, it does appear that the purpose and importance of this form of political communication will increase and should not be ignored.

Appendix A

Content Analysis Code Sheet

V1 Campaign

1. Bill Bradley
2. Al Gore
3. Gary Bauer
4. George W. Bush
5. Steve Forbes
6. John McCain

V2 Length   _____

V3 Contrast

1. Color

2. B&W

3. Mix

V4 Presence or absence (visual and/or verbal) of Morreale's (1993)
       presidential campaign film archetypes (check for present):

1. Candidates learn responsibility and love of country from their father, while learning religious and other core moral values from their mother.
2. Candidates have a hard-scrabble beginning in life, but succeed through hard work.
3. Candidates have a "love story" relationship with their spouse.
4. Candidates are good with their children and/or grandchildren.
5. Candidates come from "small town America."
6. Candidates are athletic.
7. Candidate is modern Cincinnatus, concerned with duty to country.
8. Candidates display wartime heroism.
9. Candidates are associated with political party heroes of the past
10. Candidates have the power to restore the "American Dream" that has been temporarily lost.
11. Other _____

V5 Presence or absence (visual and/or verbal) of Roberts's (1993)
       symbolic roles in presidential TV ads (check for present):

1. The Great Communicator (Gives a speech, press conference, talks with voters)
2. Chief Visionary (Talks about the future, dream, destiny, space)
3. Hero (Large crowds cheering, working late in office, war hero, medals, honors)
4. Father Figure (With children, with family, photos of family in office)
5. Chief Budget Setter (Talks about economy, taxes, inflation, prices, welfare)
6. Official Keeper of American Values (Mentions rights, freedom, equality, peace)
7. Commander-in-Chief (Seen with armed forces, domestic riots, law enforcement)
8. Chief Legislator (Address Congress, meet congressional leaders, propose bill)
9. World Leader (With foreign leaders, signing treaties, talks about world peace)

10. Chief Educator (Appearing as a role model in an educational/training situation)
11. Other _____

V6 Does the videocassette most closely resemble an "image" or an "issue" ad, according to Garramone's (1986) definition: *Issue ads* spend more time outlining the candidate's policy stands, show the candidate speaking directly to voters in a "talking head ad," use simpler production techniques, and use language which is more specific. *Image ads,* on the other hand, spend more time playing up the candidate's personal qualities, show the candidate in action with family or supporters, use more complex production techniques, and use language that is more general, which allows for more inferences to be made by the viewer.

1. Predominantly *image* oriented
2. Predominantly *issue* oriented
3. Truly balanced, no predominance

V7 Does the video meet the definition of a "documentary film" as defined by the Academy of Motion Picture Arts and Sciences ("Documentary films are defined as those dealing with historical, social, scientific, or economic subjects, either photographed in actual occurrence or re-enacted, and where the emphasis is more on factual content than on entertainment. The purely instructional film will not be considered.")?

1. Yes
2. No

V8 Who is seen in the candidate's video?

1. Children
2. Senior Citizens
3. Blacks
4. Hispanics
5. Asians
6. Disabled
7. Veterans
8. Women
9. Blue-Collar Workers

10. White-Collar Workers
11. Member(s) of the candidate's family
12. Other _____

V9 What locations are used in the video?

1. Unidentifiable office
2. Oval Office
3. Their official office (congressional/governor)
4. Military setting
5. Foreign country
6. Classroom
7. Industrial
8. Athletic
9. Home
10. Rally
11. Urban
12. Rural
13. Outside Congress, inside House or Senate
14. Other _____

Appendix B

Interview Guide

1. Please tell me a little about your background in political campaign work. What other videos/TV spot ads have you done? For which candidates?
2. Tell me about your work, your title, your responsibilities for this campaign.
3. Whom did you report to in the campaign?
4. What were your instructions when you went about making the candidate's video?
5. How many people worked with you to make the video?
6. What function did the video play in your candidate's overall campaign strategy?
7. How much did the video cost to produce?
8. Tell me about these candidate videos as a method of disseminating political information. How many were made? Whom were the videos targeted to? What were the demographics of the target? Why?
9. What was the primary message that you were trying to get across to viewers? Why?
10. What verbal messages in the video did you want to stand out the most? Why?
11. What visuals in the video did you want to stand out the most? Why?
12. What effect did you want the video to have on viewers? Why?

Bibliography

BOOKS AND ARTICLES

Abramowitz, A.I., and Stone, W.J. (1984). *Nomination politics: Party activists and presidential choice.* New York: Praeger.

Allen, M. (1996, August 26). The applause-o-meter still thrives in politics; television and parties seek quick responses. *New York Times,* p. D5.

Ashley, L., and Olson, B. (1998). Constructing reality: Print media's framing of the women's movement, 1966 to 1986. *Journalism & Mass Communication Quarterly,* 75 (2), 263–277.

Avery, D.R. (1991). Advertising, 1900–present: Capitalist tool or economic necessity? In Wm. David Sloan (Ed.), *Perspectives on mass communication history* (pp. 242–258). Hillsdale, NJ: Lawrence Erlbaum Associates.

Baldasty, G. (1984). *The press and politics in the age of Jackson.* Journalism Monograph No. 89. Columbia, SC: Association for Education in Journalism and Mass Communication.

Barber, J.D. (1977). *The presidential character.* Englewood Cliffs, NJ: Prentice-Hall.

Barker, J. (1999, June 4). When McCain's not McCain. *Arizona Republic,* p. A1.

Barnouw, E. (1993). *Documentary: A history of the non-fiction film.* New York, NY: Oxford University Press.

Barone, M. (1995, December 4). A front-runner and the rest of the pack. *U.S. News & World Report,* p. 58.

Barsam, R. (1992). *Nonfiction film theory and criticism.* Bloomington, IN: Indiana University Press.

Bartels, L. (1988). *Presidential primaries and the dynamics of pubic choice.* Princeton, NJ: Princeton University Press.

Bateson, G. (1984). *Mind & nature.* New York: Bantam Books.

Becker, L.B., and McCombs, M.E. (1978). The role of the press in determining voter reactions to presidential primaries. *Human Communication Research*, 4, 301–307.

Berry, J. (1992, April 27). Selling youth on the vote. *Adweek's Marketing Week*, p. 16.

Best, K. (1990, January 31). But is it art? Republican candidates campaign with video. *St. Louis Post-Dispatch*, p. 4A.

Blockbuster (2000). Information can be found on their web site: www.block buster.com.

Blumenthal, S. (1987, July 29). Kemp's fast forward: A campaign video for the '88 candidacy. *Washington Post*, p. D1.

Brady, H.E., and Johnston, R. (1987). What's the primary message: Horse race or issue journalism? In G.R. Orren and N.W. Polsby (Eds.), *Media and momentum: The New Hampshire primary and nomination politics* (pp. 127–186). Chatham, NJ: Chatham House.

Brownlow, L. (1949). *The president and the presidency*. Chicago: University of Chicago Press.

Carlin, D.B., and McKinney, M.S. (Eds.). (1994). *The 1992 presidential debates in focus*. Westport, CT: Praeger.

Carney, J. (1999, June 28). McCain's next battle. *Time* (July 5, 1999) p. 37.

Ceaser, James W., and Busch, A. (1993). *Upside down and inside out: The 1992 elections and American politics*. Lanham, MD: Rowman and Littlefield Publishers.

Chanlor, M. (1995). The effects of televised political advertisements on candidate image. Ph.D. diss., University of Oklahoma.

Cobb, N. (1980, November 21). The boom in home video equipment. *Boston Globe*.

Cohen, R. (2000, January 20). New bipartisan poll gives Bush big lead among Hispanic voters. *The Star-Ledger*, p. 14.

Colford, S. (1994, October 10). Direct mail sophistication aids political solicitations. *Advertising Age*, p. S10.

Connolly, C. (1999, June 27). Campaign video stars a grass-roots Gore. *Washington Post*, p. A8.

Consumer Electronics Association (2000). Information can be found on their web site: www.ce.org

Cook, K. (1997, May). Mr. Smith stays in Washington. *Campaigns & Elections*, p. 23.

Cook, R. (1994, May 7). A generation of voters is up for grabs. (Column). *Congressional Quarterly Weekly Report*, p. 1166.

Cornwell, E. (1965). *Presidential leadership of public opinion*. Bloomington: Indiana University Press.

Cundy, D.T. (1990). Image formation, the low involvement viewer, and televised political advertising. *Political Communication and Persuasion*, 7, 41–59.

———. (1986). Political commercials and candidate image: The effect can be substantial. In L.L. Kaid, D. Nimmo, and K.R. Sanders (Eds.), *New perspectives on political advertising* (pp. 210–234). Carbondale: Southern Illinois University Press.

De Grazia, A. (1965). *Republic in crisis*. New York: Federal Legal Publications.

Delli Carpini, M.X., and Williams, B.A. (1994). Methods, metaphors, and media research: The uses of television in political conversation. *Communication Research*, 21(6), 782–812.

Denton, R.E., Jr., and Woodward, G.C. (1998). *Political communication in America.* Westport, CT: Praeger.

Denzin, N.K. (1988). *The research act.* New York: McGraw-Hill.

Devlin, L.P. (1994). Television advertising in the 1992 New Hampshire presidential primary election. *Political Communication*, 11, 81–99.

———. (1986). An analysis of presidential television commercials, 1952–1984. In L.L. Kaid, D. Nimmo, and K.R. Sanders (Eds.), *New perspectives on political advertising* (pp. 21–54). Carbondale: Southern Illinois University Press.

Diamond, E., and Bates, S. (1992). *The spot: The rise of political advertising on television.* 3rd ed. Cambridge: MIT Press.

DiStaso, J. (1995, August 24). Alexander likes new poll. *Manchester Union Leader,* p. 6A.

Doak, D. (1995, July). Attack ads: rethinking the rules. *Campaigns & Elections,* p. 20.

Dreher, M. (1994). Qualitative research methods from the reviewer's perspective. In Janice M. Morse (Ed.), *Critical issues in qualitative research methods* (pp. 202–221). Thousand Oaks, CA: Sage Publications.

Droppelt, J., and Shearer, E. (1999). *Nonvoters: America's no shows.* Thousand Oaks, CA: Sage Publications.

Edelman, M. (1976). Political settings as symbolism. In George N. Gordon (Ed.), *Drama in life: The uses of communication in society* (pp. 348–359). New York: Hastings House.

Entman, R.M. (1993). Framing: Toward clarification of a fractured paradigm. *Journal of Communication*, 43, 51–58.

———. (1991). Framing U.S. coverage of international news: Contrasts in narratives of KAL and Iran Air incidents. *Journal of Communication*, 41, 6–27.

Fahey, T. (1988, February 14). Primary benefits include cash and coverage. *Manchester Union-Leader,* p. 6.

Faucheux, R. (1997, June). Creative video ideas: Inexpensive ways to produce campaign messages. *Campaigns & Elections,* p. 31.

———. (1994, August). Versatile videos: Videos as political campaign tools. *Campaigns & Elections,* p. 34.

Feeney, S. (1996, January 14). Hopefuls' biographies: Whistle stops or video flops? *Dallas Morning News,* p. H8.

Fingerson, L. (1999). Active viewing: Girls' interpretations of family television programs. *Journal of Contemporary Ethnography*, 28, 389–418.

Folkerts, J., and Teeter, D. (1988). *Voices of a nation: A history of media in the United States.* Paramus, NJ: Prentice-Hall, 1988.

Friedman, R. (1973). On the concept of authority in political philosophy. In J.A. Flathman (Ed.), *Concepts in social and political philosophy* (pp. 120–146). Englewood Cliffs, NJ: Prentice-Hall.

Gamson, W. (1992). *Talking politics.* New York: Cambridge University Press.

Gamson, W.A., and Modigliani, A. (1987). The changing culture of affirmative action. In R.G. Braungart and M.M. Braungart (Eds.), *Research in political sociology* (vol. 3, pp. 137–177). Greenwich, CT: JAI Press.

Garramone, G. (1986). Candidate image formation: The role of information processing. In L.L. Kaid, D. Nimmo, and K.R. Sanders (Eds.), *New perspectives on political advertising* (pp. 235–247). Carbondale: Southern Illinois University Press.

Geer, J.G. (1986). *Assessing voters in presidential primaries.* Tempe, AZ: Arizona State University.

Ghanem, S. (1997). Filling the tapestry: The second level of agenda setting. In M. McCombs, D., L. Shaw, and D. Weaver, (Eds.), *Communication and democracy: Exploring the intellectual frontiers in agenda-setting theory* (pp. 231–248). Mahwah, NJ: Erlbaum.

Gitlin, T. (1980). *The whole world is watching: Mass media in the making and unmaking of the new left.* Berkeley: University of California Press.

Glasser, S.B. (2000, April 30). Hired guns fuel fundraising race. *Washington Post,* p. A1.

Goetzl, D. (1999, October 25). "Brand, not bio, inspires Bush's ads." *Advertising Age.* P. 1.

Goffman, E. (1974). *Frame analysis: An essay on the organization of experience.* New York: Harper & Row.

Graber, D.A. (1987). Magical words and plain campaigns. In L.P. Devlin (Ed.), *Political persuasion in presidential campaigns* (pp.185–196). New Brunswick, NJ: Transaction Books.

Grove, L. (1987, October 28). Campaigns courting voters via their VCRs. *Washington Post,* p. A7.

Habermas, J. (1976). Legitimation problems in the modern state.

Habermas, J. (1979), *Communication and the evolution of society.* Boston: Beacon Hill Press.

Hagstrom, J., and Guskind, R. (1988, January 9). Hitting the spot. *The National Journal,* p. 75.

Hastedt, G.P., and Eksterowicz, A.J. (1993). Presidential leadership in the post cold war era. *Presidential Studies Quarterly, 23,* 445–458.

Herzik, E.B., and Dodson, M.L. (1982). The presidency and public expectations: A research note. *Presidential Studies Quarterly, 12,* 168–173.

Holsti, O.R. (1969). *Content analysis for the social sciences and humanities.* Reading, MA: Addison Wesley.

Huang, K.S. (1996). A comparison between media frames and audience frames: The case of the Hill-Thomas controversy. Paper presented to annual conference of the International Communication Association, Chicago, IL.

Iyengar, S. (1991). *Is anyone responsible? How television frames political issues.* Chicago: University of Chicago Press.

Jacobs, L. (1979). *The documentary tradition.* New York: W.W. Norton.

Jamieson, K.H. (1996). *Packaging the presidency.* New York: Oxford University Press.

———. (1988). *Eloquence in an electronic age: The transformation of American speechmaking.* New York: Oxford University Press.

BIBLIOGRAPHY 117

Jervis, Robert (1997). *System effects: Complexity in political & social life.* Princeton, NJ: Princeton University Press.
Jewell, M.E. (1974). A caveat on the expanding use of presidential primaries. *Policy Studies Journal,* 2, 279–284.
Johnson-Cartee, K., and Copeland, G. (1997). *Manipulation of the American voter: Political campaign commercials.* Westport, CT: Praeger.
Joslyn, R. (1986). Political advertising and the meaning of elections. In L.L. Kaid, D. Nimmo, and K.R. Sanders (Eds.), *New perspectives on political advertising* (pp. 139–183). Carbondale: Southern Illinois University Press.
———. (1980). The content of political spot ads. *Journalism Quarterly,* 57, 92–98
Just, M.R., Crigler, A.N., Alger, D.E., Cook, T.E., Kern, M., and West, D.M. (1996). *Crosstalk: Citizens, candidates and the media in a presidential campaign.* Chicago: University of Chicago Press.
Just, M.R., Crigler, A.N., and Wallach, L. (1990). Thirty seconds or thirty minutes: What viewers learn from spot advertisements and candidate debates. *Journal of Communication,* 40(3), 120–133.
Kahn, K.F., and Greer, J.G. (1994). Creating impressions: An experimental investigation of political advertising on television. *Political Behavior,* 16, 93–112.
Kahneman, D., and Tversky, A. (1984). Choice, values, frames. *American Psychologist,* 39, 341–350.
Kaid, L.L. (1997). Effects of the television spots of images of Dole and Clinton. *American Behavioral Scientist,* 40, 1085–1091.
Kaid, L.L., and Davidson, D.K. (1986). Elements of videostyle: Candidate presentation though television advertising. In L.L. Kaid, D. Nimmo, and K.R. Sanders (Eds.), *New perspectives on political advertising* (pp. 184–209). Carbondale: Southern Illinois University Press.
Kaid, L.L., and Sanders, K.R. (1978). Political television commercials: An experimental study of type and length. *Communication Research,* 5, 57–70.
Kaid, L.L., Chanslor, M., and Hovind, M. (1992). The influence of program and commercial type on political advertising effectiveness. *Journal of Broadcasting & Electronic Media,* 36, 303–318.
Kakutani, M. (1998, March 1). Portrait of the artist as a focus group. *New York Times Magazine,* p. 26.
Kendall, K. (2000). *Communication in the presidential primaries: Candidates and the media, 1912–2000.* Westport, CT: Praeger.
Kennamer, J.D. (1990). Comparing predictors of the likelihood of voting in a primary and a general election. *Journalism Quarterly,* 67, 777–784.
Kern, M. (1989). *30-second politics: Political advertising in the eighties.* New York: Praeger.
Kern, M., and Just, M. (1995). The focus group method, political advertising, campaign news and the construction of candidate images. *Political Communication,* 12, 127–145.
Key, V.O., Jr. (1956). *American state politics.* New York: Knopf.
Kiernan, L. (1987, August 2). C-TV: Candidates on video. *Boston Globe.*
Koeppel, D. (1992, March 2). The high-tech election. *Adweek's Marketing Week,* p. 18.
Koplinski, B. (2000). *Hats in the ring.* North Bethesda, MD: Presidential Publishing.

Kosicki, G.M. (1993). Problems and opportunities in agenda-setting research. *Journal of Communications*, 43, 100–127.

Kranish, M. (1999, July 25). Presidential hopefuls vie in N.H. with varied spending tactics. *Boston Globe*.

Krugman, D.M. (1985). Evaluating the audiences of new media. *Journal of Advertising*, 14, 21–27.

Krugman, D.M., Shamp, S.A., and Johnson, K.F. (1991). Video movies at home: Are they viewed like film or like television? *Journalism Quarterly*, 68, 120–131.

Kurtz, H. (1995, September 27). Dole personal reintroduction. *Washington Post*, p. A4.

Lacayo, R. (1998, March 16). All the president's movies. *Time*, p. 72.

Lambro, D. (1999, November 8). More minorities claim to vote as independents. *Insight on the News*, p. 32.

Lang, A., and Lanfear, P. (1990). The information processing of televised political advertising: Using theory to maximize recall. *Advances in Consumer Research*, 17, 149–158.

Lardner, J. (1987). *Fast forward Hollywood, the Japanese & the battle over the VCR*. New York: W.W. Norton.

Lehigh, S. (1998, June 7). On-screen performances display power of candidate videos. *Boston Globe*, p. A23.

Len-Rios, M.E. (2000). A case study of the Bush and Gore web sites "En Español": Building identification with Hispanic voters. Paper presented at the 2000 Convention of the Association for Education in Journalism and Mass Communication, Phoenix, Arizona.

Levy, M. (1989). *The VCR age*. Thousand Oaks, CA: Sage Publications.

Lichter, R.S., Noyes, R.E., and Kaid, L.L. (1997). No news or negative news: How the networks nixed the '96 campaign. In L.L. Kaid, and D.G. Bystrom (Eds.), *The electronic election: Perspectives on the 1996 campaign communication* (pp. 142–156). Mahwah, NJ: Lawrence Erlbaum Associates.

Lincoln, Y.S., and Guba, E.G. (1985). *Naturalistic inquiry*. Beverly Hills, CA: Sage Publications.

Lindlof, T.R. (1995). *Qualitative communication research methods*. Thousand Oaks, CA: Sage Publications.

Lonetree, A. (1993, April 6). St. Paul mayoral candidate on a roll: Video becomes new campaign tool. *Minneapolis Star Tribune*, p. 6B.

Lowden, N.B., Andersen, P.A., Dozier, D.M., and Lauzen, M.M. (1994, June). Media use in the primary election: A secondary medium model. *Communication Research*, 21, 293–304.

Loza, E. (1988). Business, amigo? No! Amigo business? Si! *Public Relations Journal*, 44, 8.

Lunt, P., and Livingstone, S. (1996, Spring). Rethinking the focus group in media and communication research. *Journal of Communication*, 79.

Luntz, F.I. (1988). *Candidates, consultants, and campaigns: The style and substance of American electioneering*. New York: Basil Blackwell.

Magleby, D.B. (2000). *Getting inside the outside campaign*. Edited by David B. Magleby. A report of a grant funded by the Pew Charitable Trusts.

Maher, M. (1995). Population: The once and future environmental crisis. In L. Chiasson, Jr. (Ed.), *The press in times of crisis* (pp. 201—218). Westport, CT: Praeger.

Maltese, J. A. (1994). *Spin control.* Chapel Hill, NC: University of North Carolina Press.

Marchand, R. (1985). *Advertising the American dream.* Berkley, CA: University of California Press.

Marks, P. (2000, February 11). Mrs. Clinton ready for her close-up and attuned to how it's used. *New York Times,* p. B7.

Matlack, C. (1992, March 7). We have met the anomie and he is us. *National Journal,* p. 600.

Matthews, C. (1988). *Hardball: How politics is played.* New York: Summit Books.

McCracken, G. (1988). *The long interview.* Qualitative Research Methods Series. Thousand Oaks, CA: Sage Publications.

McKinney, M.S., and Lamoureux, E.R. (1999). Citizen response to the 1996 presidential debates: Focusing on the focus groups. In L.L. Kaid, and D.G. Bystrom (Eds.), *The electronic election: Perspectives on the 1996 campaign communication* (pp. 10–27). Mahwah, NJ: Lawrence Erlbaum Associates.

Meckler, L. (2000, October 23). Democrats attack Bush record in Texas in new video. Associated Press.

Milkis, S.M., and Nelson, M. (1994). *The American presidency: Origins and development.* Washington, D.C.: Congressional Quarterly Press.

Milne, J. (1987, November 2). Candidates reach out to N.H. voters via video. *Boston Globe.*

Misciagno, P. (1996). Rethinking the mythic presidency. *Political Communication,* 13, 329–344.

Morgan, D. (2000, May 2). A made-for-TV windfall. *Washington Post,* p. A1.

Morgan, D.L. (1997). *Focus groups as qualitative research.* 2nd ed. Qualitative Research Methods Series. Thousand Oaks, CA: Sage Publications.

Morgan, T. (1985). *FDR: A biography.* New York: Simon and Schuster.

Morreale, J. (1994a). The Bush and Dukakis convention campaign films. *Journal of Popular Culture,* 20, 141.

———. (1994b). American self images and the presidential campaign film, 1964–1992. In Arthur H. Miller and Bruce E. Gronbeck *(Ed.) Presidential campaigns and American self images* (pp. 150–167). Boulder, CO: Westview Press.

———. (1993). *The presidential campaign film: A critical history.* Westport, CT: Praeger.

———. (1991). *A new beginning: A textual frame analysis of the political campaign film.* Albany, NY: State University of New York.

Moseley, M. (1999, April 4). Young Americans volunteer but don't vote. (Column) *Campaigns & Elections,* p. 35.

Mott, F.L. (1941). *American journalism: A history of newspapers in the United States through 250 Years, 1690 to 1940.* New York: Macmillan.

Muir, J.K. (1995). Review of *The presidential campaign film. Presidential Studies Quarterly,* 25, 154–156.

Mundy, A. (1995, October 23). Controlling the spin to win. *Mediaweek,* p. 22.

Neuman, R.W., Just, M.R., and Crigler, A.N. (1992). *Common knowledge: News and the construction of political meaning.* Chicago: University of Chicago Press.

Nicholson, J. (1999, October 30). George W. Bush begins ad splurge. *Editor & Publisher,* p. 35.

Nimmo, D. (1987). Elections as ritual drama. In L.P. Devlin (Ed.), *Political persuasion in presidential campaigns* (pp.159–173). New Brunswick, NJ: Transaction Books.

Norrander, B. (1988). *Super Tuesday: Regional politics & presidential primaries.* Lexington, KY: University of Kentucky Press.

————. (1986). Presidential primary voters as a subset of general election voters. *American Politics Quarterly,* 14, 35–53.

Norrander, B., and Smith, G.W. (1985). Type of contest, candidate strategy, and turnout in presidential primaries. *American Politics Quarterly,* 13, 28–50.

Novak, J.M. (1997). Hope springs eternal: The reinvention of America in Bill Clinton's 1996 campaign biography video. *American Behavioral Scientist,* 40, 1049–1057.

————. (1995) Narrative construction of leadership in the 1992 campaign biography film of George Bush and Bill Clinton. Ph.D. diss., Pennsylvania State University.

Oldfield, D.M., and Wildavsky, A. (1989). Reconsidering the two presidents. *Society,* 26, 54–59.

Oppenheimer, B.I. (1996). The importance of elections in a strong congressional party era: The effect of unified vs. divided governments. In B. Ginsberg and A. Stone (Eds.), *Do elections matter?* 3rd ed. (pp. 120–139). Armonk, NY: M.E. Sharpe.

Page, C. (1993, July 27). Search for remedies keeps running into wall of America's guilt avoidance. *Houston Chronicle,* p. A13.

Pan, Z., and Kosicki, G.M. (1993). Framing analysis: An approach to news discourse. *Political Communication,* 10, 55–5.

Parmelee, J. (2000). Presidential primary 2000 videocassettes: A framing study. Paper presented at the National Convention of the Association for Education in Journalism and Mass Communication, Phoenix, Arizona.

Pauly, J.J. (1991). *A beginner's guide to doing qualitative research in mass communication.* Journalism Monograph No. 125. Columbia, SC: Association for Education in Journalism and Mass Communication.

Pfau, M., and Burgoon, M. (1989). The efficacy of issue and character attack message strategies in political campaign communication. *Communication Reports,* 2, 53–61.

Pfau, M., Diedrich, T., Larson, K.M., and Van Winkle, K.M. (1995). Influence of communication modalities on voters' perceptions of candidates during presidential primary campaigns. *Journal of Communication,* 45, 122.

————. (1993). Relational and competence perceptions of presidential candidates during primary election campaigns. *Journal of Broadcasting & Electronic Media,* 37, 275–292.

Pollard, J.E. (1947). *The presidents and the press.* New York: Macmillian Company.

Popkin, S.L. (1991). *The reasoning voter: Communication and persuasion in presidential campaigns.* Chicago: University of Chicago Press.

Power: Hardball. (1988, April). *Regardie's Magazine,* p. 195.

Price, V., Tewksbury, D., and Powers, E. (1997). Switching trains of thought: The impact of news frames on readers' cognitive responses. *Communication Research*, 24, 481–506.

Putnam, R.D. (1992). *Making democracy work: Civic traditions in modern Italy.* Princeton, NJ: Princeton University Press.

Ranney, A. (1977). *Participation in American presidential nominations: 1976.* Washington, D.C.: American Enterprise Institute.

———. (1972). Turnout and representation in presidential primary elections. *American Political Science Review*, 66, 21–37.

Reynolds, J.K. (1989, November). The VCR: very critical resource. *Direct Marketing*, 52, 7, p. 51.

Rhee, J.W. (1997). Strategy and issue frames in election campaign coverage: A social cognition account of framing effects. *Journal of Communication*, 47 (3), 26–48.

Riffe, D., Lacy, S, and Fico, F. (1998). *Analyzing media messages: Using quantitative content analysis in research.* Mahwah, NJ: Lawrence Erlbaum Associates.

Roberts, C. (1981). From primary to the presidency: A panel study of images and issues in the 1976 election. *The Western Journal of Speech Communication*, 45, 60–70.

———. (1979). Media use and difficulty of decision in the 1976 presidential campaign. *Journalism Quarterly*, 56, 794–802.

Roberts, M.. (1993). Exploring the symbolic roles of the modern presidency in campaign commercials: 1952–1988. Paper presented to the Advertising and Marketing Section of the 1993 Popular Culture Conference, New Orleans, Louisiana.

Roberts, M., and McCombs, M. (1994). Agenda setting and political advertising: Origins of the news agenda. *Political Communication*, 11, 249–262.

Robinson, M.J., and Sheehan, M.A. (1983). *Over the wire and on TV.* New York: Russell Sage Foundation.

Roefs, W. (1998). From framing to frame theory: A research method turns theoretical concept. Paper presented at the 1998 Convention of the Association for Education in Journalism and Mass Communication, Baltimore, Maryland.

Rollins, P. (1997, January). Hollywood's presidents, 1944–1996: The primacy of character. *World & I.*, 56–67. [Article can be found on Internet at http://h-net2 .msu.edu/~filmhis/presidents.html],

Ronald Reagan weekly radio addresses: The president speaks to America. (1987). Wilmington, DE: Scholarly Resources.

Rosenstiel, T. (1992, January 8). Candidates hope to turn on voters via campaign videos. *Los Angeles Times*, p. A5.

Rosenthal, A. (1990). *Writing, directing and producing documentary films.* Carbondale, IL: Southern Illinois University Press.

Sabato, L., and Beiler, D. (1988). Magic … or blue smoke and mirrors? Reflections on new technologies and trends in the political consulting trade. In J. Swerdlow (Ed.), *Media technology and the vote: A source book* (pp. 1–16). Boulder, CO: Westview Press.

Sabato, L.J. (1981). *The rise of political consultants.* New York: Basic Books.

Scammell, M. (1990). Political advertising and the broadcast revolution. *The Political Quarterly*, 61, 200–213.

Scheufele, D.A. (1999). Framing as a theory of media effects. *Journal of Communication*, 49, 103–122.

Schneider, P. (1996). Social barriers to voting. *Social Education*, 25, 355.

Sherr, S.A. (1999). Scenes from the presidential playground: An analysis of the symbolic use of children in presidential campaign advertising. *Political Communication*, 16, 45–59.

Shyles, L.C. (1986). The television political spot advertising: Its structure, content, and role in the political system. In L.L. Kaid, D. Nimmo, and K.R. Sanders (Eds.), *New perspectives on political advertising* (pp. 107–138). Carbondale, IL: Southern Illinois University Press.

————. (1984). The relationship of images, issues and presentational methods in televised spot advertisements for 1980's American presidential primaries. *Journal of Broadcasting*, 28, 405–421.

Sloan, J.W. (1996). Meeting the leadership challenges of the modern presidency: The political skills and leadership of Ronald Reagan. *Presidential Studies Quarterly*, 26 (3), 795–804.

Sloan, W.D. (1991). *Perspectives in mass communication history*. Hillsdale, NJ: Lawrence Erlbaum Associates.

Speckman, K. (1999). The 1996 presidential nomination contests: Network news coverage. Paper presented to the annual meeting of the Association for Education in Journalism and Mass Communication, New Orleans, Louisiana.

Spragens, W.C. (1989). Transitions in the press office. In J. Pfiffner and R.G. Hoxie, *The presidency in transition*. New York: Center for the Study of the Presidency.

Startt, J.D., and W.D. Sloan (1989). *Historical methods in mass communication*. Hillsdale, NJ: Lawrence Erlbaum Associates.

Stempel, G.H., III. (1981). Statistical designs for content analysis. In G.H. Stempel III and B.H. Westley (Eds.), *Research methods in mass communication* (pp. 132–143). Englewood Cliffs, NJ: Prentice-Hall.

Tait, P. (1994, December). Eight myths of video cassette campaigning. *Campaigns & Elections*, p. 34.

Taylor, P. (1999). *Tennessean* editor appears in Gore campaign video. Article can be found on Web: www.freedomforum.org/professional/1999/8/4sutherland.asp.

————. (1987, June 18). Pitch for labor vote finds tough critics. *Washington Post*, p. A1.

Taylor, R.E., Hoy, M.G., and Haley, E. (1996). How French advertising professionals develop creative strategies. *Journal of Advertising*, 25, 1–14.

Thompson, J., and Kuhnhenn, J. (1995, November 5). GOP courts Florida. *Kansas City Star*, p. A1.

Thorson, E., Christ, W.G., and Caywood, C. (1991). Effects of issue-image strategies, attack and support appeals, music and visual content in political commercials. *Journal of Broadcasting & Electronic Media*, 35, 465–486.

Timmerman, D.M. (1996). 1992 presidential candidate films: The contrasting narratives of George Bush and Bill Clinton. *Presidential Studies Quarterly*, 26, 364.

Trent, J.S. (1978). Presidential surfacing: The ritualistic and crucial first act. *Communication Monographs*, 45, 281–292.

Trent, J.S., and Friedenberg, R.V. (1995). *Political campaign communication.* Westport, CT: Praeger.

Troy, G. (1996). *See how they ran: The changing role of the presidential candidate.* Cambridge: Harvard University Press.

Tucker, L.R. (1998). The framing of Calvin Klein: A frame analysis of media discourse about the August 1995 Calvin Klein Jeans advertising campaign. *Critical Studies in Mass Communication,* 15, 141–157.

Vennochi, J. (1987, September 20). Pols dish out satellite stew, candidates offering videos, free satellite links to television news. *Boston Globe.*

Video production group forms local chapter. (1985). *Washington Post,* Washington Business section, p. F21.

Walker, M. (1992, February 17). Clinton claws his way back via videos. *Guardian,* p. 26.

Walter, D. (1999). Nonbroadcast video. In D. Perlmutter (Ed.), *The manship school guide to political communication* (pp. 196–200). Baton Rouge, LA: Louisiana State University Press.

Washington Notebook (1995, September 27). Dole releases campaign video. *Dayton Daily News,* p. 7A.

Webb, E.J., Campbell, D.T., Schwartz, R.D., and Sechrest, L. (1966). *Unobtrusive measures: Nonreactive research in the social sciences.* Chicago: Rand McNally.

West, D.M. (1997). *Air wars: Television advertising in election campaigns, 1952–1996.* Washington, D.C.: Congressional Quarterly Press.

Wolburg, J.M., and Taylor, R. (1998). Rethinking the unintended consequences: The pursuit of individualism in primetime television advertising. Paper presented at the 1998 Convention of the Association for Education in Journalism and Mass Communication, Baltimore, Maryland.

Woo, J. (1996). Television news discourse in political transition: Framing the 1987 and 1992 Korean presidential elections. *Political Communication,* 13, 63–80.

Wye, M.J. (1996). From Hyannisport to Hollywood: A critical theory approach to the development of the presidential bio film in modern politics. Ph.D. diss., University of Southern California.

VIDEOCASSETTE AND INTERVIEW REFERENCES

Alexander, Lamar. 1995., "Lamar!" Produced by Mike Murphy, Washington, D.C. Videocassette, produced by Murphy, Pintak, Gautier, Hudome. Falls Church, Virginia

Bauer, Gary. 1999. "Who I Am and What I Believe." Produced by Edmonds Associates, Washington, D.C. Videocassette.

Bradley, Bill. 1999. "People Are Talking." Produced by MacWilliams, Cosgrove, Smith, Robinson, Washington, D.C. Videocassette.

Bush, George W. 1999. "A Fresh Start." Produced by Maverick Media, Austin, Texas. Videocassette.

Clinton, Bill. 1991. "The New Convenant." Produced by Clinton campaign. Videocassette, produced by Great American Media, Inc., Washington, D.C.

Curcio, Paul. (2001). Telephone interview with author, January 3, 2001.

Dole, Bob. 1995. "Bob Dole: An American Hero." Produced by Stuart Stevens, Washington, D.C. Videocassette. Produced by the Stevens and Schriefer Group, Washington, D.C..

Edmonds, Tom. (2001). Telephone interview with author on January 3, 2001.

Forbes, Steve. 1999. "A Rebirth of Freedom." Produced by Our Town Films, Bernardsville, New Jersey. Videocassette.

Gore, Al. 1999. "The Al Gore Story." Produced by Squire, Knapp, Dunn Communications, Washington, D.C. Videocassette.

Gramm, Phil. 1995. "Gramm: Restoring the American Dream." Produced by Alex Castellanos, Washington, D.C. Videocassette, produced by National Media Inc., Alexandria, Virginia.

Kerrey, Bob. 1991. "Nebraska at Its Best: Bob Kerrey, A Personal Profile." Produced by Kerrey campaign. Videocassette.

Knapp, William. (2001). Telephone interview with author on January 21, 2001.

McCain, John. 1999. "The Character to Do What's Right, the Courage to Fight for It." Produced by Stevens, Reed, Curcio and Company, Alexandria, Virginia. Videocassette.

Robertson, Pat. 1987. "Pat Robertson: Who Is this Man?" Produced by Robertson campaign. Videocassette.

Sanderson, Paul. (2001). Telephone interview with author on January 26, 2001.

Simon, Paul. 1987. "The Paul Simon Story." Produced by Simon campaign. Videocassette.

Index

Dreher, Melanie, 5
Dukakis, Michael, 1988 presidential primary video of, 19

Edelman, Murray, 63
Edmonds, Tom, 15, 89–90, 95
Entman, Robert, 6, 27–28

Faucheux, Ron, 62
Florida Democratic straw poll, 1991, 19–20
Florida Republican straw poll, 1995, 22
Forbes, Steve, 2000 presidential primary video of: family values, 40; flat tax, 41, 66; Mikhail Gorbachev, 77; individual freedom, 40–41; medical savings accounts, 41; privatizing Social Security, 41; Margaret Thatcher, 40
Frame analysis, 27–28
Friedman, Richard, 60

Garramone, Gina, 58, 64
Gitlin, Todd, 6, 27–28
Gore, Al, 2000 campaign film of: Gore's relationship with his wife, 50; mental health care, 51, 83; values, 50–52, 78; presidential primary video of: educational reform, 67; environment, 32; family history, 31; Tipper Gore, 33–34; humor, 32–34; President Clinton endorsement, 33; John Seigenthaler, 45; small-town values, 31–34; Vietnam War, 31, 72
Graber, Doris, 60–61
Gramm, Phil, 1996 presidential primary video of, 23
Greer, Frank, 20
Grove, Lloyd, 16–18

Harkin, Tom, 1992 presidential primary video of, 21
Image-based vs. issue-based appeals, 57–58, 64–68
In-depth interviews, 85–87
Iyengar, Shanto, 5

Jamieson, Kathleen, 82
Joslyn, Richard, 58

Kahneman, Daniel and Tversky, Amos, 48
Kaid, Lynda L. and Davidson, Dorothy K., 60
Kaid, Lynda L. and Sanders, Keith R., 58
Kemp, Jack, 1988 presidential primary video of, 17–18
Kendall, Kathleen, 7
Kerrey, Bob, 1992 presidential primary video of, 21
Klein, Joe, 20
Knapp, William, 87–88, 94, 96–97
Koeppel, Dan, 21–22

Letterman, David: in 1996 Bob Dole primary video, 24; in 2000 Al Gore primary video, 32
Lindlof, Thomas, 85
Lugar, Dick, 1996 presidential primary video of, 22–23

Marchand, Roland, 12
Maseng, Mari, 17–18
McCain, John, 2000 presidential primary video of: campaign finance reform, 44–45, 66; Cindy McCain, 43–44; political courage, 44–45, 76; Social Security, 44; values, 42–44, 69–70; Vietnam War, 43–43, 66–67, 72
McCracken, Grant, 85–86
McCurry, Mike, 21
Morreale, Joanne, 6, 58–59
Mundy, Alicia, 2, 24
Murphy, Mike, 22

Nimmo, Dan, 61

Page, Clarence, 19
Pauly, John, 5
Political advertising, 6–9, 12–14
Political communication and the media, 8

About the Author

JOHN H. PARMELEE is an Assistant Professor of Communications at the University of North Florida. Before joining the academic world, Parmelee was a reporter for *Congressional Quarterly* and *Kiplinger's Personal Finance Magazine.*